USING DOCUMENTS

Ian Davies ● Chris Webb

ENGLISH HERITAGE

CONTENTS

BELOW: A scene of distress in London's East End, 1912. There is a wealth of evidence here, from family size to their clothes, and in the detail such as the handful of pawn tickets in the man's hand. Is this a picture of reality or one the photographer has created?

Hulton Deutsch

ABOUT THIS BOOK

The past is all around us and in recent years there has been a great deal of work on how teachers and pupils can use oral history, artefacts, and other sources. Surprisingly, though, there has been relatively little attention to one of the most obvious and significant ways in which the past can be understood: namely through an analysis of documentary evidence.

This book aims to fill that gap and to suggest ways in which teachers can introduce their pupils to the delights of working with the written records of the past. The challenge is to find ways of introducing these sources to pupils in such a way that they have a clear understanding of both the language that is used and the context in which sources are written; that they are given real historical exercises to undertake and encouraged to begin to develop their own interpretations of sources by developing sophisticated analytical skills; and to know something about the way in which records are kept so that further investigations will be possible.

This book

■ introduces teachers and pupils to archives which are readily available for all parts of England

■ encourages pupils to get the most from archives, providing suggestions for activities of general application and of application to each specific source

■ works within the framework of the National Curriculum for pupils aged 5-16

■ provides ideas for work with pupils and students and others undertaking activities not directly related to the National Curriculum

■ gives explanations about a number of key historical themes (such as poverty, work, leisure) referring at all times to the ways in which records relating to them can be accessed.

GREAT OAKLEY is a village and parish, on Ramsey Creek, a feeder of the Stour, and on the road from Colchester to Harwich, 5 miles north from Thorpe-le-Soken station on the Colchester and Walton-on-the-Naze line, and 4 south from Wrabness station on the Harwich and Manningtree branch of the Great Eastern railway, 6 south-west from Harwich, 7 south-east from Manningtree, 14 from Colchester and 65 from London, in the North Eastern division of the county, hundred, petty sessional division and union of Tendring, Harwich county court district and in the rural deanery of Ardleigh and Harwich, archdeaconry of Colchester and diocese of St. Albans. The church of All Saints is an ancient building of stone and brick, partly Norman and consisting of chancel and nave and a belfry containing one bell : in the nave is a tablet to the Rev. Richard Drake M.A. rector here 1718, who erected an almshouse for four aged women of the parish : there is a fine Norman font of polished marble, supported on five stone shafts : the church was restored in 1880, when the galleries were removed and the pews replaced by open benches at a cost of £400, defrayed by general contributions ; during the progress of the work a large flag stone was discovered, in with a marble slab bearing an inscription to Sarah ell, daughter of Thomas Savell, of Great Oakley, *ob.* 16th ch, 1619 : there are sittings for 250 persons. The re-r dates from the year 1559. The living is a rectory, age tithe rent-charge £687, with residence and 57 acres ebe, in the gift of St. John's College, Cambridge, and

Documentary evidence exists in many forms, from handwritten parchments to photographs.

TOP RIGHT: From Kelly's Directory of Essex 1895.

LEFT: Well-to-do Victorian children in about 1860. Compare this with the photograph on the inside back cover.

BELOW: John Wesley (1703-91), the founder of the Methodist Society preaching to an unsympathetic crowd at Wednesbury, Staffordshire.

Each section is devoted to a particular theme. One or more record sources have been chosen to illustrate the theme. The records are discussed in relation to the background which led to their creation, and the consequences or implications of their existence. Next comes a section on activities suitable to the records discussed. There is also information on locating the records and a list of other records related to the theme under discussion.

HOW TO USE DOCUMENTS IN THE CLASSROOM

The following points should help you to present documentary evidence to pupils with confidence:

■ Do not use records in isolation. They should be used in a context which is limited but which pupils find challenging. Records should add to pupils' understanding of an historical period or topic rather than merely provide opportunities to add variety to lessons.

■ Ensure that each exercise using source material has clear objectives to encourage pupils to go beyond an uncritical reading of the text.

■ Avoid questions which will only result in pupils becoming frustrated. Constantly asking pupils, for example, if a source is primary or secondary, may mean that pupils come to feel that this can be regarded as an end point. Of course, the establishment of whether a source is secondary or primary should lead pupils to consider other factors such as its usefulness or its reliability.

■ Try to avoid presenting pupils with too many or too few sources. Obviously the most appropriate number will vary depending upon individual circumstances. Similarly, the way in which sources are presented to pupils will be important. As a general rule there is a direct relationship between the complexity of the language of a source and the level of understanding that can be developed when using that source. The easier the language level, the more potential a source has for developing complex historical understanding. For some this issue will raise certain difficulties in that it may imply that sources should be tampered with to improve access: teachers must be aware of the degree to which they can alter a source before its historical value is lost altogether.

Mike Corbishley

■ A variety of sources should be used. Teachers should be wary of concentrating exclusively on written material.

■ Consideration needs to be given to the way in which sources are introduced to pupils. Many teachers and many textbooks introduce records by means of an explanation which pupils come to regard not simply as one of many possible approaches, but as the sole truth which must be respected. While pupils do find the establishment of an initial framework useful, teachers should encourage a critical approach to be taken to all material in the classroom. This initial framework should be of an appropriate length and involve an appropriate level of thought: too much 'interesting' but essentially irrelevant background 'colour' may only serve to mislead pupils.

RELIABILITY AND BIAS

Pupils will find it useful to be challenged on a number of misconceptions. The most common of these are:

■ Eyewitness accounts must be reliable

■ Contemporary accounts must be eyewitness accounts

LEFT: Many families have an archive of personal records.

■ Secondary sources are less reliable than primary sources

■ Secondary sources are less useful than primary sources

■ Reliable sources must be useful

■ Biased sources must be useless

■ Reliable sources must be unbiased

■ Biased sources must be unreliable

■ The 'truth' lies automatically somewhere between two conflicting sources.

The number of sources which make a certain point should be accepted as the only factor needed in deciding on the correctness of a certain view:

■ A reliable source gives the historian an accurate view of what was happening generally across all geographical areas and all social classes and both genders.

■ There is a fundamental difference between primary and secondary sources which means that a source is categorically one or the other, irrespective of the use an historian is making of that source.

■ There is no difference between the notion of bias and that of inaccuracy.

■ The word reliable is used only to show that a source is regarded as showing an accurate perception and cannot be used to show that a particular (but mistaken) view was commonly held among a certain group of people in the past.

PLANNING LESSONS AND SCHEMES OF WORK

The National Curriculum statutory orders are the obvious starting point for most teachers, but it would be unwise to attempt to cover all areas of work.

Determining precisely how the topic is limited involves a consideration of a number of factors, some of which relate to what might be termed 'educational objectives' and some to more practical matters. One possible planning sequence is as follows:

■ Consult statutory guidelines to ascertain what must and what could be done. The main focus will be on the key elements of the Programmes of Study.

■ Outline some of the key elements which are felt to be significant.

Some relevant ideas here could be that the unit should be based on an issue-based problem solving approach rather than on a narrative. An overarching question could be investigated by the pupils. For example, using documents for different aspects of the Industrial Revolution you could focus pupils' attention by asking, 'Did standards of living improve during the period 1750-1800?'.

This question will allow pupils to establish an initial hypothesis at the beginning of the unit which will be modified throughout the time that pupils are working on the topic. Pupils should also

■ have the opportunity to learn about the experiences of both men and women

■ use a range of historical sources both in terms of type (for example written documents and maps) as well as those which allow pupils to consider both local and national issues

■ undertake historical enquiry which develops understanding and skills relating to the study of history.

RIGHT: A variety of documentary and pictorial sources from one family.

USING PRIMARY MATERIAL

Which primary material should be used? There is no simple answer to this question, because there are so many variables involved:

■ What part of the curriculum is being studied?

■ What are the age groups and abilities of the pupils?

■ How much time is there for preparation and study?

However, there are a number of useful approaches. First, there are many good guides to primary sources (see Bibliography). They are not expensive and make good additions to a library. They will tell you what sorts of records are available generally, and something about their nature, purpose and interpretation.

Second, some repositories publish packs of facsimiles aimed either at specific topics or at specific groups of records. These can be used either as packs in the classroom or as a teacher's guide to the kind of sources available for a particular topic.

HOW TO LOCATE PRIMARY MATERIAL

Nowhere in England is very far from a source of primary material. Printed editions of important texts have been published since the seventeenth century, with national and local record societies being formed in great numbers in the nineteenth century. As a result, vast quantities of primary material are available in print, with consequent advantages for accessibility both in geographical terms and in terms of greater ease of use. This latter is particularly important for periods earlier than the eighteenth century when deciphering handwriting can become a problem.

Another significant advantage of using printed material is that it can often be borrowed, or bought and used in the classroom or at home. Furthermore, a good edition should have an introduction which can be enormously helpful in giving information about the source, its origins, purpose and pitfalls in compilation and interpretation.

If primary material has not been printed, or it is important to use it in its original form, access need not be difficult. Every pre-1974 county and all but Avon of the post-1974 counties in England have a county record office, usually located in the county town. In addition there are many district record offices, particularly in the metropolitan counties, and specialist repositories run by universities, businesses and other organisations. Local libraries often also have original primary material, sometimes in original form, sometimes as microfilm or other copies, in addition to being a source of printed primary material.

Getting access to primary material

The facilities provided by record repositories vary widely, but all have an area (usually called a search room) in which individuals can study the documents in their care. Some repositories insist on prior appointments to study records, others welcome searchers without prior notice. Some are open only during office hours, but many open one or more evenings in the week or on Saturdays. Information on opening hours and other conditions is given in *British Archives: A Guide to Archive Resources in the United Kingdom* (see Bibliography). But for teachers it is always wise to contact the repository beforehand, for two main reasons:

■ teachers are likely to require more detailed and specialist advice than is normally available, and prior notice alerts the repository to this need.

■ some repositories have members of staff whose particular remit includes education (some repositories have teachers seconded to them) and it makes sense to take advantage of this facility if it is available.

All repositories can photocopy records, but in most this is done by staff rather than searchers and will not be carried out while you wait. It is important, therefore, to plan well ahead if copies are required for use in class. In addition, archivists will not allow documents to be photocopied if there is any risk of damage to the documents. Archivists have to bear in mind the needs of the public of the future, not just of today. In these cases a photograph will often be offered as a substitute, but this might be too expensive for the needs of the project.

WORKING ON THE RECORDS

In taking notes from records all repositories will insist that only pencils can be used. This sounds an irritating restriction, but it is not unknown for ball-point or fountain pen ink to find its way onto a document, with consequent avoidable work for hard-pressed conservators. When tracing maps, searchers are often asked to place a melinex (or similar) sheet between the map and the tracing paper, to protect the map from possible damage. Maps are often too large to copy by any other method, and it might be necessary to make a specific appointment to ensure that a large enough table is available.

Preparing for a visit

Preparation beforehand is important, because it nearly always saves valuable time. For example, it would be pointless to visit a repository with the single idea of working on enclosure in Anyvillage if upon arrival at the repository it was discovered that the Anyvillage enclosure took place long before the eighteenth-century enclosure acts, with a consequent lack of local documentation. Similarly, visiting a repository to find 'anything at all

MARCH 27 1869

PEABODY-SQUARE,
WESTMINSTER.

These buildings were completed last Christmas, and were fully occupied at the beginning of the new year. They are on the north side of Victoria-street, and are surrounded by Little Chapel-street, Brewer's-green, Palmer's-passage, and Brewer's-green-passage. The square is composed, with one open side, of three detached blocks, averaging 100 ft. long, 32 ft. wide, and 46 ft. high from the ground to the eaves of the roof. These blocks altogether contain ninety-three dwellings, or 225 rooms, and a board-room for the meetings of the trustees.

ABOVE: **Primary material for the Peabody Trust available in facsimile form in a teaching pack. (see Bibliography page 36).**

English Heritage Education Service

English Heritage Education Service

LEFT & ABOVE: Pupils from Queen Anne's School, York, studying documents at the Borthwick Institute, York.

on the history of Anytown' would be equally fruitless. Information overload will be the inevitable result, and will produce frustration for both searcher and staff.

Preparation can take the form of a phone call or a letter to the repository, but whichever is chosen, a well informed contact will always invoke a much better response, simply because it is easier to give advice to someone who is clearly not starting from first principles.

Preparing students

It is particularly important to do some ground work before students embark on individual projects. One of the most common complaints of archivists is that pupils turn up, unannounced, with little knowledge, expecting individual tutorials on their chosen projects. Archivists are more than willing to offer advice and guidance, but should not be expected to act as surrogate tutors for students.

Archivists know the records, but they cannot know what is expected of students by the curriculum or the exam, and cannot know what might be appropriate for an individual. It is not uncommon for students to wish to tackle subjects which are beyond their abilities and begin to flounder too late to make any changes. Contact with the repository by the teacher beforehand can nearly always prevent these problems arising.

Finding the records

During the course of a visit, the staff will direct searchers to the documents relevant to each enquiry, and should also be able to offer advice on the origins, purpose and interpretation of documents consulted. However, if at all possible, it is a good idea to spend some time browsing through the finding aids provided. Most repositories contain many millions of individual documents, so that no archivist, however knowledgeable, can possibly know more than a small fraction of the documents in his or her care. Finding aids should, however, help to guide the searcher to the right place.

The arrangement of archives and the documents within them is a complicated and time consuming business, so that many archives have significant listing backlogs. Unlike books, documents cannot be catalogued according to a well-

defined and pre-determined scheme. Much of the importance of a document lies in its relationship to other documents. For example, the significance of a deficit shown in one year of a firm's accounts can only be judged in terms of a whole series of accounts for the same firm. Was this a bad year, or was it merely the latest in a long line of deficits? If it was the first deficit, did it coincide with the death, retirement or other removal of a key member of staff? The point is an obvious one, yet it has profound implications for the arrangement of records.

Archivists do not see records as single entities, but merely as component parts of the greater whole. The cataloguing unit for an archivist is the archive, (ie, all the records created by or received by a single organisation) not the individual record.

Similarly, the place in which a record was created, or the place to which it refers, is not so important as the organisation which created it. In practical terms, this means that searching for records relating to Anytown will almost certainly not be confined solely to records or archives with Anytown in their titles. Thus, if Anytown was a part of the Blacktown Poor Law Union it will be necessary to look at the list of Blacktown Poor Law Union records, or if the major manufacturer was a branch of Exemplar Chemicals, based 500 miles away in Cornwall, then one should not expect to find much of relevance locally.

Finding aids

Finding aids take various forms. The main point of access to documents is the list, which can be more or less detailed according to its purpose. Most lists are indexed

and some repositories have computerised many, if not all of their lists and indexes, so that searching through them can be a quick and relatively painless exercise. Again, though, it is important to be as specific as possible in the use of lists and indexes. Information overload is a real danger, which should be avoided at all costs.

USING THE RECORDS WITH PUPILS

Once the records have been located and identified a decision has to be made about whether to use them in class in copy form, to use the originals, or to send pupils to use them as individuals in their own projects.

■ Copying depends on the facilities available and the nature of the documents, but should not present problems in most cases. Where it is wished to make further copies from those provided by the repository it is best to work out an agreement for doing so.

■ Some repositories have classrooms or lecture rooms, and will welcome visits by school or college groups. Other repositories might be willing to take documents to local schools or colleges and conduct a class themselves.

■ Project work by individual pupils usually presents the most difficult problems, but most repositories will be willing to talk about arrangements to overcome timetabling and other logistical difficulties. It is often best to arrange a group visit by all project students before they start their research. This can sort out all the little questions, such as how to order records and making appointments, which arise in each individual case.

HOUSING AND LIFESTYLE

THE BACKGROUND

What one person considers within the term lifestyle can differ radically from another. Here it means the everyday existence of people, including in particular their housing conditions and the objects they had and used around them on a daily basis. As the definition of lifestyle can be wide or narrow according to one's choice, so the sources for studying lifestyle can be drawn from an almost infinitely wide range. Here we shall look at probate inventories, themselves of such manifold variety that in the space available it is impossible to do more than scratch the surface.

THE CONSEQUENCES

Probate inventories are lists of moveable goods drawn up by appraisers after a person's death and submitted to a probate court in the course of proving a will or seeking a grant of administration. They survive in some places from the fourteenth century, but they exist most abundantly in the sixteenth, seventeenth and eighteenth centuries. They decline in quality and quantity in the second half of the eighteenth century, but in a few places they are available into the nineteenth century.

At their most basic, inventories simply record the goods remaining in the deceased's possession. But in the best examples they locate these goods in named rooms in the deceased's house, and, in the case of rural dwellers, often record crops growing or gathered into the barns, together with any livestock.

Inventories survive for all sorts of people and virtually all social levels. They are by no means confined to the rich, and indeed, it is often the rich who are missing from the records. They have usually sorted out their affairs long before death, or had such complicated sets of possessions that the formal requirement to produce an inventory was overlooked by the probate court. Nevertheless, one can expect to find more inventories for the mid-

Interior of a Victorian sitting room.

Mary Evans Picture Library

dling sort, (for example, yeomen and shopkeepers) than for labourers. Similarly men are better represented than women, although spinsters and widows are more common than one might imagine, and it is worth noting that it is not true that married women could not make wills - it was difficult for them, certainly, but not impossible.

LOCATING THE RECORDS

Probate was predominantly in the hands of ecclesiastical courts (although there were a few secular exceptions to this rule). Each diocese had at least one probate court (often called a consistory court) under the jurisdiction of the bishop, and one or more courts under 'peculiar' jurisdictions, often under the authority of the dean and chapter of the cathedral.

In some dioceses, (York, for example) there could be many of these peculiars. The practice was that a will should be proved by (or in the case of dying without leaving a will, administration should be sought from) the court with jurisdiction over the place where the deceased's goods were to be found, not where the deceased died. Clearly, this could lead to difficulties with individuals who were so wealthy as to have goods in more than one ecclesiastical jurisdiction, with consequent potential for conflict between courts over which should have the business (and therefore the fees) of proving the

will. To avoid this difficulty the concept of *bona notabilia* developed. In essence this meant that where a deceased person's goods lay in more than one jurisdiction, the will or administration became the proper concern of the archbishop's court (Canterbury in the southern province and York in the northern). If goods were split between the two provinces then Canterbury took precedence over York. However, in practice this neat theory might be overlooked by courts eager to take fees and by executors looking for convenience, so some creative thinking and digging might be necessary if you wish to locate the records of a particular individual.

Each probate court kept its record in different ways, and the records have certainly fared very differently since coming into the hands of (mainly county) record offices. Methods of searching for records from particular places will vary so much that the best advice is to ask for guidance in each individual repository.

As well as looking at conventional inventories, it can be worth while exploring the records of disputed wills. Again, the church courts were the first and principal port of call for people who wished to dispute a will or contest the actions of executors. As a result the consistory court records are full of detailed evidence files (cause papers), often under-exploited, which can include detailed inventories and executors' accounts.

OTHER RECORDS

■ wills

■ ecclesiastical court records of tithe, defamation and matrimonial disputes

■ diaries

■ newspapers.

STUDYING AN INVENTORY

There follows a transcription of an inventory (right) of an unmarried serving woman who lived in the reign of Elizabeth I. Jane Curle probably occupied a single room in the household of her mistress. Her possessions were few, and included few luxuries apart from her best gown (a gift from her mistress) and a couple of silver spoons. Jane certainly slept in this room (she has a mattress, a pillow and coverlets) and probably cooked and ate in it too (pewter dishes, cooking pots and a frying pan). The absence of a reference to a fire could be because its associated equipment (for example, landirons and spits) was the property of her mistress and so not valued amongst Jane's own possessions. She has plenty of storage for her clothes, which are more commonly valued as a lump sum together with money in cash rather than individually itemised as here. Jane (and/or her mistress) clearly valued her appearance.

The reference to cattle (kye) at the end of the inventory is a reminder of the 'rural' character of even an important and large city like York in the sixteenth century, with cattle, pigs and hens being kept in yards at the back of houses and shops. Jane's two kye, however, could have been kept outside the city as part of a larger herd. The fact that she was to have the increase of them for two years suggests that they were a legacy or gift and not part of the normal possessions of a woman of her position.

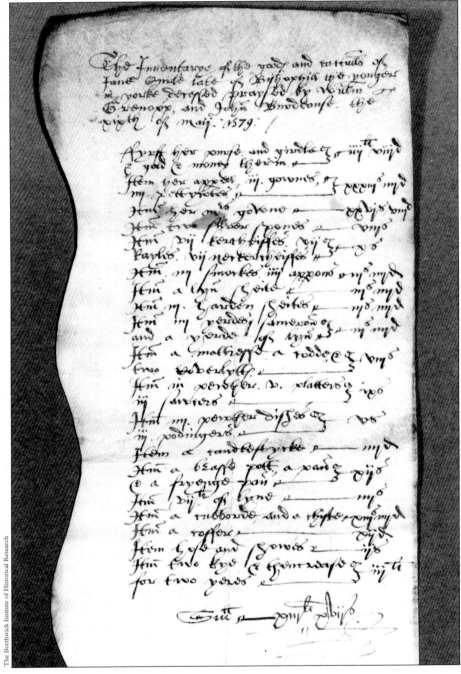

The Borthwick Institute of Historical Research

The Inventarye of the goodes and cattalls of Jane Curle late of Bishophill the yonger in Yorke decessed praysed by William Grenopp and John Burdeouse the xixth of Maij 1579

Fyrst her purse and girdle
and gold and money therin
iiijli viijd

Item her apparell iij gownes
iiij pettycotes
xxxiijs iiijd

Item her Mistress gowne
xxvjs viijd

Item two silver spones
viijs

Item vij kercheiffes vij
Rayles vij neckercheiffes
xs

Item iiij smockes iiij apperons
iijs iiijd

Item a lynin sheite
iijs iiijd

Item iij harden sheites
iijs iiijd

Item iiij yerdes sameron
and a yerde of lynin
iijs iiijd

Item a mattresse a codde and
two Coverlyttes
viijs

Item in pewther v platters
iij sawcers
ixs

Item iiij pewther dishes
iij podingers
vs

Item a candlestycke

iiijd

Item a brasse pott a pan
and a fryenge pan
xijs

Item vijli of lyne
iiijs

Item a cubborde and a chiste
xiijs iiijd

Item a coffer
xijd

Item hose and showes
ijs

Item two kye and thencrease
for two yeres
iij li

Summa xiijli xvijs

ACTIVITY: READING DOCUMENTS

One of the most obvious, important and yet most difficult tasks for pupils to undertake is actually to *read* the documents from the past. There are conflicting views about what teachers should do to help pupils over this hurdle. For some it does not really matter if the teacher, or somebody else, transcribes and perhaps translates the document for pupils. This would mean perhaps that words are changed and in effect a new document is produced which allows pupils to develop important historical skills such as analysis leading to a greater understanding of the past.

For others, this modification of sources is defeating much of the purpose of history: it does not allow work from an original document, it will not reveal the document's true potential nor will pupils get a proper understanding of the past. There are well known examples of translations (for example, the modern as opposed to the King James version of the Bible and the original and the contemporary presentations of the Canterbury Tales). Strong views exist about what has been gained or lost.

Perhaps there is, as always, some room for compromise. Much of the decision about what to do with historical documents rests on the reason why they are being used with pupils. The age and ability of the particular groups of pupils and individuals together with their levels of motivation will signal what is possible in specific circumstances. The educational purpose of the activity also will have an impact on the nature of the best way forward: does the exercise actually require pupils to undertake the translation for themselves because teachers want them to learn to read documents and to see for themselves how communication was undertaken, or can the work be done equally well in modern English?

Read documents in the original version

Introduce the document, explaining the sort of purpose it had and its main features. This could be done diagrammatically so that there is a template or cover which could be placed over the document highlighting the main sections. Teachers will need to decide whether this template is placed over the original document, or a transcribed and typed version of it. There will also be a need to consider if that template contains questions and instructions or perhaps even help with particular words.

For the document showing the possessions of Jane Curle the simple version of the template could be quite straightforward:

■ Title and introduction which gives the name of the deceased person, and the names of those who drew up the document.

■ The list of personal goods, together with their value.

■ Goods listed by the room in which they were located, together with their value.

ABOVE: Cartoon 'Sunday at Home in 1870'.

RIGHT: 'Over London by rail'. Engraving of terraced houses by Gustave Doré in 1870.

BELOW: Kitchen 1957.

Assistance could be given for some pupils with the meaning of key terms or words that appear in the document. The amount of help that needs to be given here will obviously depend on the pupils who are working on the material. This can be done in a number of ways:

■ Help with the meaning of words that are in use today and which still mean virtually or exactly the same as they did when the document was produced (eg 'late' to mean deceased; 'indifference' to mean disinterest).

■ Help with words that are spelled slightly differently from those that mean the same today (eg 'mattresse'; 'lynin'). Often it will be worthwhile here to give pupils some general guidelines rather than focus on every individual word. For example, 'y', 'i' and 'e' on the

one hand and 'u' and 'v' on the other are often used interchangeably and an 'e' is often added at the end of a word.

■ Letters are often repeated and some may need to be ignored. Attempts should be made to read words phonetically at first to give an indication of what the writer is trying to say.

■ Roman numerals can give the reader some clues (if used flexibly and imaginatively) when using numbers.

■ Not too much attention should be paid to the use of capital letters as they were often used more freely than today.

■ There may be a need to give assistance with words that have changed their meaning or more likely with those that are have fallen from use (eg 'podingers'; 'dublettes').

Preparatory activity

It important that pupils who read the documents are encouraged to go much further than a simple vocalisation of individual words. They need to understand what those words meant and so some activity or question is needed to focus their attention. You could devise a scheme for recording the possessions of a person. Pupils should consider how to describe goods and how to come to a reasonable judgement about their value. This could be done with a number of real objects in front of pupils.

Questions associated with the activity could be:

■ Are your descriptions accurate - can another pupil recognise the object from your description? How much faith can we place in documents that describe historical objects?

■ How accurate is your valuation? Would it be possible for this to be challenged? Who might wish to challenge a valuation as being too high, or one that was seen as being too low?

■ How much are we likely to learn about a person on the basis of descriptions of possessions and

their financial valuations? Would it be necessary to probe the sentimental or personal value put on these objects and if so how could this be done?

Transcribing the document

Ask your pupils to:

■ Look over the whole document using the template described above to try to get a 'feel' for what has been written.

■ Make a list of those words which they do not understand. Use a dictionary and the guidelines given above and ask for help from other pupils in the group or the teacher if necessary.

■ Read for the sense of a sentence or entry rather than becoming bogged down trying to follow every single word.

After the transcription

Activities after transcribing the document could be to:

■ Draw a plan of the house occupied by the person who owned the objects which are described here.

■ Make comments about the sort of items that are described - what sort of furniture, clothes, cutlery etc was contained in this person's house? It would be helpful if a table could be established here to allow pupils to make comments about, for example, the level of comfort or technology that is demonstrated by the document.

■ What sort of person owned the objects that are described here? The judgement that is made must be supported by reference to the articles that are described.

LEFT: Nineteenth-century flats in Barrow-in-Furness.
BELOW: A view of a country village, early this century.
BOTTOM: Furniture catalogue of about 1890.

Mike Corbishley

Mike Corbishley

Mary Evans Picture Library

DRAWING-ROOM SUITE, No. 3.   IN AMERICAN WALNUT OR FUMIGATED MAHOGANY.

HEALTH

THE BACKGROUND

Prior to the formation of the National Health Service, many separate organisations dealt with health and disease. Under the old Poor Law, paupers might receive payment for medical care from the overseers of the poor. The new Poor Law of 1834 developed a pauper medical service and workhouse infirmaries.

In the larger urban centres, charitable hospitals and dispensaries were founded from the early eighteenth century onwards, providing in and out patient care for the 'deserving poor' who could not otherwise afford to pay for medical treatment.

Serious problems of public health arose in the nineteenth century with massive population growth and increasing urbanisation. The great cholera epidemic of 1831-2 prompted a series of national and local measures to deal with the worst effects of bad sanitation and disease. Thereafter, the organisation of public health at national and local level grew piecemeal but steadily. The 1848 Public Health Act set up a national supervising body for the first time, the General Board of Health, which had the power to establish local boards of health where necessary. Some localities appointed their own 'Medical Officer of Health'(usually a local doctor) to oversee their public health measures. The 1872 Public Health Act created urban and rural sanitary authorities and made it compulsory for every such authority to appoint a Medical Officer of Health.

THE CONSEQUENCES

The functions of the Medical Officer of Health and his staff were steadily increased in the late nineteenth and early twentieth century to include responsibility for a wide range of personal health and sanitary services. These included

■ the prevention of 'nuisances' (ie environmental health)

■ the inspection of and responsibility for the health aspects of housing

■ the fight against infectious disease and tuberculosis

■ welfare schemes for mothers and babies

■ the medical inspection of schoolchildren

■ the superintendence of municipal hospitals.

The reports of the Medical Officer of Health provide a fascinating insight into all aspects of the health of a community.

Topham Picture Library

ABOVE: An operation at Charing Cross Hospital around 1910.

BELOW: From the York Medical Officer of Health's report for July 1900.

The Borthwick Institute of Historical Research: York Health Archives

WHOOPING COUGH.

There were 47 deaths due to this very fatal infantile affliction. Of these 12 occurred in Bootham District, 7 in Micklegate District, and 28 in Walmgate District.

21 occurred in the first quarter of the year.			
16	„	second	„ „
7	„	third	„ „
3	„	fourth	„ „

MEASLES.

The number of deaths in 1897 was 28.

„	„	1898	„ 36.
„	„	1899	„ 7.
„	„	**1900**	„ **40.**

The disease occurred almost entirely during the first five months of the year, and in Micklegate and Walmgate Districts.

SMALL-POX.

During 1900 the City and neighbourhood remained entirely free from this disease.

SCARLET FEVER.

During the year 1900, 325 cases were notified, 167 of which were received into the Fever Hospital (see Table III.), or nearly 50 per cent. There were 4 deaths, all of which occurred in the Fever Hospital.

Cases notified in
{ 1897 .. 270; deaths, 1; cases received into Fever Hospital, 96.
1898 .. 364; „ 8; „ „ 133.
1899 .. 200; „ 4; „ „ 105.

Whilst the disease has been chiefly of a mild type—as is usual nowadays—so mild that many cases have been carelessly or ignorantly overlooked, and have so maintained the more or less continuous run of cases, yet there has been a larger proportion of severe cases.

LOCATING THE RECORDS

Medical Officers of Health reported to their employing body - the rural or urban sanitary authority - which, in urban places, might be a municipal borough or a local board of health or an improvement commission. In rural places it would be either the whole or part of an existing poor law union. Later, smaller communities came under Urban or Rural District Councils. The Medical Officer of Health would report to the relevant committee (eg the sanitary or the health committee). He might also, for some of his roles, have to report to another committee, for example to the education committee for the medical inspection of schoolchildren and the school medical service.

The annual reports of the Medical Officers of Health were, by the early twentieth century, usually printed. They might also be summarised in local newspapers. Copies of annual reports should be found amongst the records of the relevant local authority. Copies can often be found in local libraries (where newspapers can also usually be found). Reports vary in detail, and those for the larger towns and cities are particularly rich. Sometimes the local Medical Officer of Health also produced special reports on various topics, which were also printed.

OTHER RECORDS

Records of the overseers of the poor and records of the Boards of Guardians (after 1834) cover pauper health services, including workhouse hospitals. For towns, the records (eg the minutes) of relevant bodies, and committees, dealing with health, exist from the nineteenth century onwards. Hospital records may be accessible if they have been deposited in a local record office. However, the records of patients are closed to the public for 100 years.

ACTIVITY: ASKING QUESTIONS

Was the health of the population improving during the early twentieth century?

Teachers have always wanted to encourage pupils to have a clear understanding of key historical

The Borthwick Institute of Historical Research: York Health Archives

CITY OF YORK.
TABLE IV. (CORRESPONDING TO LOCAL GOVERNMENT BOARD'S TABLE IV.)
Causes of, and ages at, Death during the Year 1909
(Shorter Schedule B of Incorporated Society of Medical Officers of Health, extended)

No.	Causes of Death.	Deaths in whole City, at subjoined ages, of Residents, whether occurring within or without the City.						
		All ages.	Under 1 year.	1 to 5 years.	5 to 15 years.	15 to 25 years.	25 to 65 years.	65 & upwards.
1	Small-pox	nil	...	...	...	...	...	...
2	Measles	4	...	3	1	...	...	...
3	Scarlet Fever	1	...	1	...	...	...	...
4	Diphtheria and Membranous Croup	6	...	2	4	...	...	...
5	Whooping Cough	14	5	9	...	...	...	...
6	Enteric Fever	3	...	...	...	1	2	...
7	Zymotic Diarrhœa (Epidemic or Zymotic Enteritis)	17	14	1	...	...	1	1
8	Enteritis	11	8	...	...	...	1	2
9	Epidemic Influenza	6	...	...	...	1	1	4
10	Erysipelas	2	...	...	...	...	2	...
11	Puerperal Fever	1	...	...	...	1	...	...
12	Other Septic Diseases	9	...	...	1	...	7	1
13	Tuberculosis of Meninges	18	2	5	7	3	1	...
14	Tuberculosis of Lungs 115	90	1	...	6	2	59	2
15	Other forms of Tuberculosis	7	1	2	...	1	2	1
16	Cancer	73	...	...	1	1	46	25
17	Premature Birth 98	44	44	...	...	...	...	...
18	Developmental Diseases	54	53	1	...	...	...	...
19	Infantile Convulsions	27	23	4	...	...	...	...
20	Croup (False, Laryngismus)	nil	...	...	...	...	...	...
21	Old Age	82	...	...	...	...	4	78
22	Meningitis	14	7	4	...	1	2	...
23	Inflammation and Softening of Brain	9	...	...	...	...	3	6
24	Apoplexy (Cerebral Hœmorrhage)	71	1	...	...	...	24	46
25	Insanity	6	...	...	...	...	4	2
26	Spinal Cord, Diseases of	7	...	...	...	...	5	2
27	Organic Diseases of Heart and Syncope	115	...	1	2	...	62	50
28	Acute Bronchitis and Laryngitis 86	46	20	7	...	2	6	11
29	Chronic Bronchitis	40	...	...	...	1	10	29
30	Lobar (Croupous) and Lobular (Broncho)-Pneumonia	66	19	23	1	...	11	12
31	Diseases of Stomach	12	2	...	1	2	5	2
32	Obstruction of Intestines	5	...	...	...	...	2	3
33	Appendicitis	4	...	2	...	...	2	...
34	Peritonitis, general	3	...	...	1	...	2	...
35	Nephritis and Bright's Disease	38	...	...	3	1	27	7
36	Tumours and Other Affections of Female Genital Organs	2	...	...	...	...	2	...
37	Cirrhosis of Liver	6	...	...	...	...	6	...
38	Alcoholism	2	...	...	...	...	2	...
39	Accidents & Diseases of Parturition	5	...	...	...	1	4	...
40	Rheumatic Fever	4	...	...	...	...	4	...
41	Congenital Syphilis	4	2	1	...	...	1	...
42	Diabetes Mellitus	5	...	...	...	...	5	...
43	Deaths by Accident or Negligence	27	3	4	6	2	9	3
44	Deaths by Suicide	3	...	...	...	...	3	...
45	Deaths from Ill-defined Causes	6	...	...	...	...	4	2
46	All other Causes	25	1	1	1	1	15	6
	ALL CAUSES	994	206	71	35	41	346	295

concepts which will allow them to answer questions like the one above. To come to terms with such a question, pupils need to understand many aspects of history including concepts of change, continuity, cause, motivation and effect. This can be very challenging

for pupils as these concepts can be seen as rather general headings which can be sub-divided to include other matters. Change, for example, can be seen to demand an understanding of progress and regression; cause encompasses an understanding of short term, long term, separate and interrelated factors comprising webs of causation and so on.

If pupils were to use the sources for health on these pages so as to begin to attempt an answer to the question above, the following may be useful activities:

■ Pupils could classify the sorts of diseases/illnesses/disabilities that are mentioned in the documents. Which of those mentioned are infectious, non-infectious, severe, mild, affect particular age groups (eg children, old people)?

■ What types of action are being taken according to the documents (or should be taken) to attempt to improve matters generally and in relation to particular illnesses? The action might be public health action or scientific action.

■ Who could take action to improve the situation and is there any evidence from the documents that such action is being taken by

the individual who is affected
the politician
the scientist
the teacher
the employer
any others?

Once pupils have considered these questions, they should be in a position to answer the main question above. It will not be a simple matter of saying yes or no but rather answering in relation to

■ types of people

■ types of illnesses

over a particular period of time. It should be possible for them to consider the potential as opposed to the actual improvement or deterioration and whether this was intended or not. Finally, pupils should be able to pinpoint what other sources may be required to give a better answer than they have been able to make so far.

RIGHT: The New Asylum, Colchester about 1905.

ABOVE: The York Medical Officer of Health's report of 1912.

The Borthwick Institute of Historical Research: York Health Archives

---

141

THE DISPOSAL OF EXCREMENT AND REFUSE.

The scavenging and sewerage of the City are under the control of the City Surveyor, and to him I am indebted for some of the following facts :—

The methods in vogue in the City consist of :—

(1) About 3,930 midden-privies (a steadily diminishing number) the contents of which are removed systematically once a month by and at the cost of the Corporation. The manure is sold to farmers, part being forwarded from the City by rail.

(2) About 12,000 wash-down water-closets and 2,000 waste water-closets. The provision of the latter is now discouraged.

(3) About 14,000 ashtubs and galvanised iron receptacles (or ashbins) in use at houses where there are water-closets and no brick ashpits or midden privies. The contents are collected by the scavengers twice a week and destroyed in a Manlove and Alliot's Refuse Destructor of six cells, which consumes about 50 tons of refuse per working day, and produces about 17 tons of clinker per day. The heat generated works the day load at the Electric Light and Power Station of the Corporation.

During the 30 years ending December 31st, 1902, 2,454 midden-privies had been substituted by water-closets voluntarily or by order of the Sanitary Authority, under either Section 91 or 36 of the Public Health Act. Since the end of 1902, 2,598 midden-privies have been substituted by water-closets in similar manner, making a total of 5,052.

Measures are constantly taken, under Section 36 of the Public Health Act, to secure the provision of proper iron ashbins (with covers), in lieu of wooden boxes, old tins, and other leaky and lidless receptacles.

LABORATORY WORK.

During the year the following work was carried out in the Medical Officer of Health's Laboratory, and at the Yorkshire Pathological Laboratory, Leeds :—

Sample of effluent analysed	1
Samples of River waters analysed	5
Samples of Well waters analysed...	3

The New Asylum, Myland, Colchester.

Norman Jacobs

POVERTY

THE BACKGROUND

The records produced by poverty are voluminous. Many were created by authority in an attempt to control the poor. The legislation relating to settlement and removal is complex and was subjected to various changes. However, from the late seventeenth century until 1834 it provided, in essence, that:

■ a parish was responsible for maintaining its own poor through a poor rate levied by the overseers of the poor elected by the ratepayers for each parish

■ an adult male's parish was defined as his place of birth, unless he obtained work in another parish for more than 12 months

■ an adult female's parish was her place of birth if she was a spinster, or her husband's parish of settlement if she was married

■ children's parishes of legal settlement followed that of their parents.

As a result of this a parish could remove people who fell into poverty to their parish of legal settlement. In order to do this the overseers had to arrange for the examination of each pauper before Justices of the Peace to determine the place of settlement. After the examination the Justices would order the removal of the pauper to his or her place of settlement.

After 1834 the New Poor Law operated on the principal of 'less eligibility'. Outdoor relief was to be replaced by indoor relief in workhouses, but the conditions in the workhouses were to be so unattractive that people would not seek relief unless they were absolutely forced to do so. The administration of the Poor Law was removed from the overseers of the poor of each parish and transferred to newly created Poor Law Unions, groups of parishes under the control of a Board of Guardians, financed by a poor rate levied within each constituent parish of the Union.

THE CONSEQUENCES

Records of settlement and removal reveal poignant and telling stories, for example:

On 28 April 1803 it was found 'Upon complaint...that Jonathan Dickinson, Agnes his wife and Hannah their daughter aged nine months did lately come to Kirby Lonsdale not having gained a legal settlement there...and that [they] are...become chargeable to... Kirby Lonsdale...we the said Justices of the Peace...do...adjudge that the lawful settlement of them...is in the parish of Gosforth'.
[Cumbria Record Office, Kendal.]

The Justices of the Peace appended a note the next day saying that Jonathan was unable to travel 'by reason of sickness and great infirmity of body' so the order for removal to Gosforth was suspended. Then on 25 July 1803 the Justices expressed their satisfaction that 'the within order of removal may be executed without danger to the within named Agnes, now the widow of the above named Jonathan'. There is no further mention of Hannah.

But it was possible to move from place to place for permanent work without the fear of removal from one end of the country to another. An individual wishing to move away from home could obtain a settlement certificate, which stated that if he should fall on the poor rate of his new parish, then the expenses of supporting him would be borne by the overseers of his parish of legal settlement, for example:

'Robert Norton of Gray's Inn Lane (being the place of his last legal settlement) hath a desire to remove from our said parish of St Andrew, Holborne to Kirby Lonsdale where he hopes to find such employment that he maintain himself and family without being burthensome to any parish...so we the... overseers of St Andrew's...do...own and acknowledge the said Robert Norton...to be an inhabitant legally settled within our said parish of St Andrew...13 July 1702'.
[Cumbria Record Office, Kendal.]

LOCATING THE RECORDS

The overseers of the poor for the parish kept a copy of the settlement examination and the removal order with their own records (occasionally it turns out that both removing and removed to parishes have these records) and the Justices of the Peace caused records to be kept amongst the records of Quarter Sessions. Nearly all parish records are now deposited in the appropriate county record office. The county record office is also the home for the records of the Justices - the court of Quarter Sessions. Records of Boards of Guardians are more scattered, some finding their way to district as well as county record offices.

OTHER RECORDS

■ accounts of overseers

■ accounts and minutes of Boards of Guardians

■ dietaries (lists of food provided on a daily basis) for workhouses

■ records of charities (coal, clothing, medical etc)

■ surveys like that of Booth in London or Rowntree in York

■ correspondence and diaries of those working with the poor

■ records of pre-1834 workhouses sometimes also survive.

ACTIVITY: ANALYSING A DOCUMENT

Draw up a table or chart to allow pupils to show what they can learn about the people mentioned in the documents. The table could include various sections, for example,

Name

Single or married?

Children?

Jobs that he has done

Age?

Place of birth

Chronology

Put the documents in order. Make a special note of the dates that they were produced. Now using blank maps of the United Kingdom draw lines to show the journeys that were made by Joseph Mawson and his family. Pupils could annotate the maps to include details about the dates at which those places were reached. This may lead to questions being raised about:

■ the distances that were travelled

■ the means of transport

■ the length of time it would have taken to travel those distances

■ the possible reasons those people had for travelling to those particular places.

There could be opportunities on the basis of this work to encourage pupils to identify explicitly

■ those things which have been identified from the sources on these pages

■ those factors which have been culled from other, possibly secondary sources

■ those which are being inferred or imagined.

Comments can then usefully be made on the extent to which it is necessary or important for historians to rely on sources. The point that this sort of evidence is written by certain persons and not others (the poor are not invited to submit their account) may allow pupils to consider the usefulness of the documents.

Transcribing a document

One or more of the documents could be transcribed. Questions about the ways in which the documents have been written could be raised, for example:

■ the style of handwriting

compared with today

■ the nature of words used

■ sentence construction

■ the consistency of spelling, even of people's names.

The emphasis is generally on formality for legal documents past and present, but issues can be discussed about language use. There are many words that have changed their meaning. We have many new words today while some words have virtually disappeared. Some would argue that language would help identify people of different social status and reinforce those relative positions.

ACTIVITY: ROLE PLAY

The material on poverty lends itself very well to role play activity. It is important to establish particular questions for the class to think about. Although the experience of

the role play and its use for developing more sophisticated historical understanding among pupils would be the main goals, there would almost inevitably be some importance attached to the performance of the role play, and as much authenticity should be aimed for by using some fairly simple and straightforward techniques, for example:

■ by encouraging pupils to use appropriate vocabulary and sentence structures

■ by dressing in slightly different clothes to give an emphasis to the need to think and speak differently

■ by having a formal start and finish to the role play

■ by stressing that the pupils are dealing with important issues and that they are considering real rather than imaginary people which means that historical accuracy must be respected as far as possible.

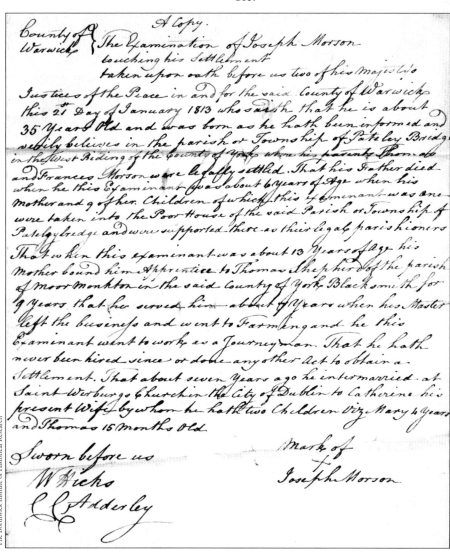

The Borthwick Institute of Historical Research

The following steps could be followed to develop a role play using the documents provided about Joseph Mawson:

■ Establish the detailed context of the role play. It could take place following the letter that was written on 10 May 1814 by Robert Tesseyman, Joseph Ware and Thomas Hinks. This would allow material from earlier incidents to be reviewed.

■ The focal point of the role play could be an investigation by a government official into the workings of the old poor law. This would give an opportunity for questions to be asked of the main characters, and for issues to be raised for class discussion following the role play.

■ As an alternative to the role of the government official, or as an additional character, one pupil could serve as a modern historian who would be gathering information for a book. The strength of using both would be that modern and nineteenth century perspectives would be raised, although some may feel that as few imaginary people as possible need to be included.

The main characters in the role play could include some or all of the following:

Joseph Mawson
Catherine Mawson (Joseph's wife)
Frances Mawson (Joseph's mother)
George Hinchliffe (Governor of the Birmingham workhouse)
W Hicks and C C Adderley (magistrates of the County of Warwickshire)
Robert Tesseyman, Robert Ware and Joseph Hicks (magistrates in the parish of Moor Monkton)
A government official investigating the workings of the poor law
A modern historian gathering material with which to write a book on poverty.

It would be important for pupils to have an opportunity to prepare their roles in detail by focusing on a number of central questions. One of the most obvious questions that could be tackled in this case would relate to the fairness of the way in which Mawson was treated. 'Were the magistrates cruel?' could be a good question to arouse interest

and to focus attention.

Throughout the role play the ways of thinking of the people of the nineteenth and twentieth centuries need to be focused on.

■ **The human cost and response to issues associated with poverty.** Pupils could talk about the plight of Mawson and his family. Where do they live at different times? What happens to the children? What sort of work did he do and try to do? The part played by his parents (particularly his mother following his father's death). Would Mawson be classed as someone who was poor in absolute or relative terms?

■ **The financial cost of relieving poverty.** What could be done to make things better even if individuals were well disposed towards

the poor? Workhouses were expensive and the burden of paying for them was distributed evenly across the country.

■ **Issues about the causes of poverty.** Pupils could ask whether this situation was Mawson's own fault or if he was the victim of circumstance? Questions relating to individual moral responsibility may be significant. The questions relating to the alleged pregnancy of a woman who was not Mawson's wife could be probed here. Was there work available at this time if Mawson had been willing (or able) to move?

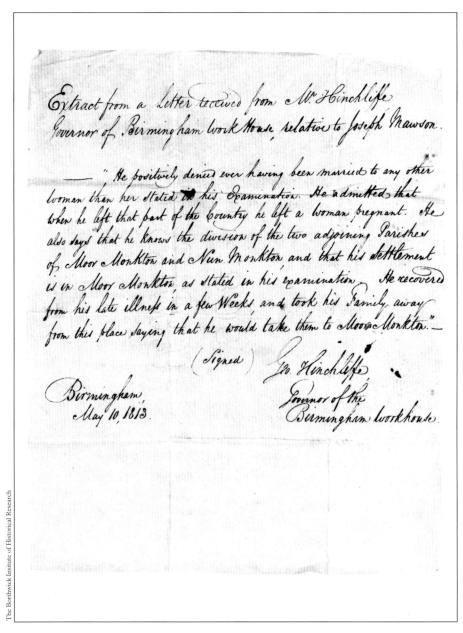

ABOVE: New ward for the casual poor at Marylebone Workhouse, 1867.

BELOW LEFT: Cartoon 'The Poor Laws, Past and Present' published in 1836.

BELOW RIGHT: Plan and drawing of a workhouse published by the Poor Law Commissioners to show Poor Law Guardians the type of workhouse which ought to be built.

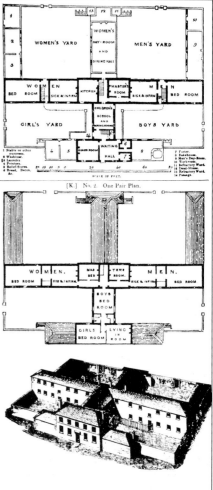

POPULATION

THE BACKGROUND

The size and dynamic of a population are two of the most important factors in reconstructing any historical community. Issues such as growth, decline and the mechanisms for them (growing birth rate, falling death rate, harvest failure, plague or disease, improved health, immigration, emigration and so on) are all questions that exercise historical demographers.

From 1801 we are fortunate to have the ten-yearly census to help us to answer these questions with some confidence about the size and dynamic of the population we are dealing with. Before 1801, however, the sources for answering even basic questions like the size of the population in a given area at a given time are less reliable and require more rigorous historical evaluation. There are a few national estimates of the population (one of the most famous being Gregory King's surprisingly accurate estimate in 1695) and many more local listings. But the most generally available source is the parish registers of baptisms, marriages and burials, kept (in theory) by each ecclesiastical parish from 1538 onwards by order of Thomas Cromwell.

THE CONSEQUENCES

Parish registers were introduced with the purpose of recording the vital events in the individual lives of Christians: baptism, marriage and burial. The registers therefore do not record population statistics directly, but can be manipulated to yield figures that approximate to populations. To construct crude total populations it is possible to compare the baptism and burial figures over a period. But baptisms are not births, and one must allow for under-registration for a variety of reasons:

■ babies born in a parish but baptised elsewhere

■ babies not baptised (through nonconformity, for example)

■ still births

■ poor record keeping by the vicar or his clerk.

Similarly, burials are not deaths, and there could again be a variety of reasons for under registration: people dying away from their home parish are the most obvious absentees. For migration studies, marriage registers are the most useful source, especially after Hardwick's Act introduced standard printed marriage registers in 1754 requiring the parties to give their place of residence at the time of marriage. The extent to which the deficiencies of registers need to be taken into account varies from parish to parish and from time to time. Statistical manipulation can help to address these problems, but local research (for example, on the extent of nonconformity) is just as valuable.

The information that each parish register contains varies greatly. In some places it is very sparse and in others it is exceptionally full. If you are lucky you might encounter the registration form devised by Rev William Dade of York in the early 1770s and used in many places in the diocese of York from Archbishop William Markham's visitation in 1777 until Rose's Act introduced standard printed forms for baptismal and burial registers nationwide in 1812. For baptisms he recorded parents and grandparents, where they came from and their occupations for each child, and for burials he recorded the deceased's occupation, cause of and age at death, and date of death and burial. There are still the generally applicable problems to overcome when using these registers, but they open themselves up to much more interesting and useful analysis than most other registers.

LOCATING THE RECORDS

As a result of the Parochial Registers and Records Measure 1979 and its recent amendment, nearly all parish registers in which the last entry is more than 100 years old, and nearly all registers which were started as a result of Rose's Act in 1812 (whether or not

they are filled) should be deposited in the appropriate record office. This is usually the county record office, but there are many exceptions to this general rule. There are also very many printed registers, which are often easier to use if the purpose is simply to construct population details. Most have been published by the appropriate county parish register society, but a good reference library or the relevant record office will be able to advise on details for each parish.

OTHER RECORDS

■ Chantry certificates (1547)

■ Compton's ecclesiastical census (1676)

■ Hearth tax returns (1660-89)

■ Poll tax returns (especially late seventeenth century)

■ Census records from 1801.

ACTIVITY: INTERPRETING STATISTICS

Investigating population trends allows for work which is full of human interest for pupils. Tables of statistical information together with the descriptive comments can give pupils the opportunity to undertake fascinating and often original historical work. Local material can allow pupils to become more knowledgeable about trends and events which may illuminate the national context as well as providing opportunities for the more obvious clarification of those issues nearer to home.

OPPOSITE PAGE
TOP LEFT: Record of Burials at St John's, Ousebridge, York 1604-5. Note entry for October 'William Young, Carryer, supposed to be strangled by his wyfe..'
BELOW LEFT: One of William Dade's registers, for 1772, showing the detail he entered for births and baptisms. TOP RIGHT: Cartoon on emigration. CENTRE RIGHT: Investigating gravestones can be a useful activity. BOTTOM RIGHT: Gravestone from Cambridge commemorating an entire family.

Births & Baptisms in 1772 — Willm Dade, Curate

Christian name	Surname	Father's name & profession	Abode	Mother's name & descent	Born	Baptized
Frances 2d child	Lakeland	Robert Lakeland, Attorney at Law, Son of William Lakeland Joyner of Kirby Ravensworth by Izabell Miller his second wife	Davygate (extraparochial)	Elizabeth eldest daughter of Daniel Francis Whisker of York, Linen Draper: descended by Francis Hargrave his first wife	twenty third of march	twenty seventh of march
Ann	Gatliff	Samuel Gatliff, working Jeweller, only son of Francis Gatliff of Girdlergate Jeweller by Ellen Thackray his wife	Stonegate	Mary daugr of Christopher Thistleton of York Tanner by Dorothy Pellatar his wife	sixth of april	thirteenth of April
William	Lochran	William Lochran, coach maker, eldest son of William Lochran coach maker by Elizabeth Hooper his wife both deceased	Davygate	Martha third daughter of mr John Brooks late Coachman, by Sarah Rhodes his wife		thirteenth of may
Mary	Robson	William Robson, whitesmith, son of Willm Robson a Groom by Mary Heborge his wife	Davygate	Ann the daughter of John Ellio, Cooper	twentieth of July	twentieth of July
Elizabeth	Firth	John Firth, Barber, son of George Firth of Appleton Farmer by Ann Ellot his wife	Davygate	Elizabeth daugr. of John Baker of Tunbridge in Kent Currier by Abigail Brisendon his wife	third of July	twenty seventh of July
William 2d son	Lee	Robert Lee Journeyman coach Maker	Swinegate		twenty second of August	twenty seventh of August
Sarah 12th Child	Grave	Benjamino Grave, Porter, Son of John Grave of Rothwell woolcomber by Mary Walker his wife	Swinegate	Ann daut of Thomas Picard of Barnby near Howden by Elizabeth Tilson his wife	ninth of October	eleventh of October
Mary illegitimate	Mitchelson	Joseph Grove the reputed Father	Davygate	Mary Mitchelson late Servant to mr. Fisher Silk mercer in Stonegate	twenty first of October	second of November
William 2d Child	Saunderson	John Saunderson, draysman, Son of Charles Saunderson of Kiveton Taylor by Ellen his wife	St Hellens Square	Ann daut of John Ripley of Acomb Labourer by Mary Blenkin his wife	fifth of november	eighth of november
Edward 2d Child	Wright	Willm Wright coat Seller, son of Edward Wright of Bishton, Butcher by Elizth Seldart his wife	Davygate	Ann daut of Ninian Procter of Scotton near Knaresbro Farmer by Ann Carr his wife	twenty fifth of November	second of December

The gravestone reads:

SARAH GREEN
DIED MARCH 1874
AND THEIR CHILDREN
Rev HENRY GREEN
MARY ANN GREEN
HARRIET MARSH
ROBERT GREEN
JAMES GREEN
EMMA MARATT

WORK

THE BACKGROUND

The modern distinctions between work and home, and work and leisure were not so marked before the end of the eighteenth century and the coming of mass employment factories heralded by Richard Arkwright's mill at Cromford in Derbyshire. Before then, dual occupation was commonplace (for example, lead mining and farming in Derbyshire, farming and spinning or weaving in the Pennine dales of Yorkshire and Lancashire) and it is therefore easy to discover sources which detail occupations and at the same time difficult to interpret the meaning of the information contained in those sources. With the advent of industrialisation, however, 'work' came to mean, in a way it had not before, paid work, and occupational descriptions came to assume more importance amongst densely populated urban areas with their highly graduated social structures.

The first census was conducted in 1801, and a similar exercise has been undertaken every decade since then (with the exception of 1941). There have been understandable changes of methodology and emphasis, but one of the main objects of census taking has been the recording of information about occupations.

THE CONSEQUENCES

From 1801-1831 the occupational information in the census was gathered by a house-to-house enquiry by the overseers of the poor or 'other substantial householders'. They were required only to record numbers engaged in the various occupational categories adopted. In 1801 these were agriculture, trade, manufactures and handicrafts and finally, other employments. The 1841 census, however, gives us for the first time on a national scale detailed, precise and comparable information, which can be matched to identifiable individuals and placed in their context of household, dwelling, street, area and town or village.

The new census enumerators who replaced the overseers and worked in districts based on the new (1837) civil registration districts, were provided with printed books in which they were required to fill in information about every individual staying in every dwelling in their particular enumeration district on the night of the census. The information gathered by the enumerators varied from census to census, but always included information on rank, profession or occupation, age, place of birth, an indication of marital status and of the size of each household.

LOCATING THE RECORDS

The census enumerators' books are in the Public Record Office in Kew, but they are so widely used at local level that microfilm copies of them are available in nearly all local authority record offices and many local history and reference libraries.

OTHER RECORDS

■ parish registers

■ trades directories

■ employment and other records of businesses

■ probate records (especially inventories).

ACTIVITY: MAKING COMPARISONS

Two of the most commonly stated purposes for studying history are that it can give pupils 'an understanding of their own cultural roots and shared inheritances' and help them 'to understand the present in the context of the past'. This section shows how pupils can use census documents to gain some understanding of work that was undertaken in the past and compare it usefully with contemporary information.

Many of the well known issues in the empathy debate can be explored in any work which compares the past with the present. Teachers may wish to consider improving pupils' work by looking for a range of responses to the past. Some pupils will present arguments as if those people from past societies were essentially the same as we are but in fancy dress. For others, those members of past societies viewed the world differently from ourselves.

Using the census

Make a census return for your own class. Pupils would have to give information about who lived in their own household on one particular night. It would be essential to undertake this activity sensitively. Teachers may have to consider the guidelines necessary for classroom enumerators. Teachers may feel that it is less important to include accurate information for a particular class than to raise issues associated with census activity. It may be possible, for example, to consider the potential that enumerators have for invading respondents' privacy. This may lead to a consideration of the accuracy of census returns in a national context. The justifications for census work and the actual usefulness of gathering this sort of information could be discussed. The meaning that these events in relation to the changing power of the national state could be raised. The categories of information requested is another topic. For example, the assumptions surrounding the identification of the head of household could give rise to interesting discussions. Use these headings (taken from the 1851 census see left) for gathering information from the class:

Rural History Centre: University of Reading

Norman Jacobs

ABOVE: Paxman's munition factory in Colchester during the First World War.

LEFT: Soap Boiler, from The Book of English Trades and Library of the Useful Arts, London 1824.

■ Name of street and number of house

■ Name and surname of each person who live in the house for one particular night

■ Relation to the head of the family (eg head, wife, son, daughter)

■ Condition (ie married/unmarried/widow etc)

■ Rank, profession or occupation

■ Where born

■ Whether blind or deaf and dumb.

You will need to discuss the terms in the 1851 census which are unacceptable today (for example, dumb) as well as the concepts no longer used (for example, 'head of the family'). Using the information from a local census return for 1851, pupils could be asked to compile information for a particular road, and then compare it with the most recent available return, or with the information that has been gathered from the class. A number of stages would have to be undertaken:

■ make a list of the jobs mentioned in the returns

■ describe the meaning of any jobs which are unclear - some help will

be needed from teachers here. If the sheet from Scholes was used, the following explanations could be given:

fishmonger - buys and sells fish.

stocking knitter - worker who usually operated a small machine or frame produced stockings to be used by men and women.

book keeper - person who would keep records (often financial) for a business.

housekeeper - person who helped to ensure that a house and the people who lived there were well looked after.

stripper in a factory - the meaning here is unclear - it could refer to a person undertaking general labouring duties or someone who stripped textile machines clear of unwanted material.

drawer in a coal pit - person who pulled coal trucks to the surface from a mine

tarpaulin coverer - fairly obvious?

View the lists to see if any direct comparisons can be made. For example, there were two painters in this street in 1851 but five painters in the most recent information. There will probably be very few (if any) direct comparisons. Now try to group the occupations into a small number of categories related to type of work, for example

■ industry - textiles, coal etc

■ domestic - servants etc

■ commercial - book keepers

and

■ nature of work (skilled, unskilled, semi skilled)

to make comparisons.

Ask questions about the comparisons that have been made above for three main overlapping purposes:

■ Questions about the nature of work carried out by individuals. Even when the same terminology is being used, to what extent are the jobs that are being described similar? Would workers in, for example, 1851 and in the most recent information work the same hours, receive the same wages, begin and finish work at the same age and at the same hours in a normal working day. Would they enjoy the same benefits (holidays, pensions, safety etc). How might the context of the work have changed? For example, is there a trend today for example to go back to a pre industrial situation in which work is increasingly done at home rather than elsewhere? What sex were most workers?

■ Questions about the knowledge this information gives about the nature of the economy at particular times. Does the information suggest that the economy has become more industrial, more commercial, more productive less labour intensive etc ?

■ Questions which range more widely over significant social and political issues as well as encouraging thought about historical change and historical methodology. For example, has progress taken place in the period under study - if so, in what ways and how do you know? Given the changes that you have noted in this work, do you feel that you can make any guesses or predictions about how work will develop in the future - is it acceptable

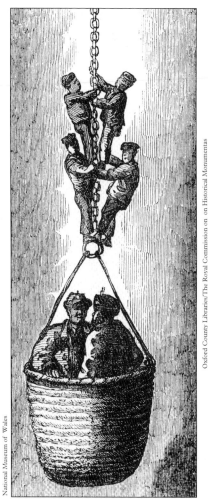

ABOVE: At work in a blanket mill, Witney, Oxfordshire in 1898.

LEFT: Coal mining. Men and boys being brought to the surface in a Welsh mine.

BELOW: A hay harvest in August 1846 published in The Illustrated London News.

for historians to make these sort of judgements or should that be left to other people (or not done at all)? Is it possible to make judgements about developments in the United Kingdom based on the work you have just undertaken? What other sources would you have to consult

before being able to answer questions associated with the reasons for the changes you have seen rather than just noting the changes themselves?

LEISURE

Norman Jacobs

Great Clacton Sunday School outing in about 1920.

THE BACKGROUND

To some people, leisure can mean merely time away from activities (often paid employment) that have to be performed. To others it means the occupation of one's time in some kind of organised activity that is both voluntary and unpaid. The key is the word organised. Organised leisure did not produce many records until the nineteenth century. As a result one has to rely on chance references in sources compiled for completely different purposes. Thus court records (both secular and ecclesiastical) might contain prosecutions of people for tippling or playing football during divine service, for attending prohibited plays (for example, mystery plays after the Reformation), while antiquarian jottings or diaries might contain references to local customs (like May Day revels or Christmas festivities). Organised leisure, in the sense of clubs, societies and so on, began to play a part in people's lives at all social levels from the nineteenth century onwards. These clubs and societies began to produce records of their own, and to advertise their existence.

THE CONSEQUENCES

It is possible to do a great deal of research on non-organised leisure activities, but these kinds of references, though existing in large numbers, are scattered throughout many different sources and so are difficult to trace without adequate time and resources. It is much easier to concentrate on the periods and kinds of activity which have left readily traceable records.

In towns, with their larger and more diverse populations one can expect to find a wide range of records of all kinds of activities. Cricket clubs, photographic societies, cycling organisations can all leave records of themselves which survive in local record offices, libraries or private hands. In addition, local newspapers are an excellent source for discovering the range of leisure activities available in a given locality.

In rural areas the opportunities for organised leisure were less diverse, but they nevertheless existed. Some rural areas were covered by good newspapers, but all too often the papers which purport to cover the countryside concentrate heavily on what went on in the main centre of population - the market towns, rather than the villages. However, from the late nineteenth century onwards villages began to rectify this difficulty by producing 'newspapers' of their own. Parish magazines were produced by the parish church (denominations other than the Church of England also produced magazines, but they tend not to survive in such large numbers at local level) and so reflect the bias of the church. They do not give a complete picture of the leisure activities available to villagers, but they do show what sort of activities were approved of and encouraged.

LOCATING THE RECORDS

Parish magazines are kept with the parish records, usually in the county record office. They can also be found in local history libraries. Newspapers are kept by libraries, record offices and newspaper offices.

OTHER RECORDS

■ diaries

■ secular and ecclesiastical court records

■ records of clubs and societies

■ trades directories

■ ale-house licensing records.

ACTIVITY: RELIABILITY
Developing an understanding of reliability

Reliability is one of the key features of historical understanding that pupils need to appreciate. For many pupils, sources and evidence are the same thing and bias, accuracy and truth are all mixed together.

Reliability can be seen in two main ways. Is a source reliable because:

■ it has been collected by reliable procedures (for example a national census return)?

■ the views it represents are reliable (for example, are the activities in Appleton-le-Street typical nineteenth-century leisure activities?)?

Bias

In addition to these considerations pupils may wish to consider the nature of bias which can be seen both by omission and inclusion. Authors may insert a positive view of an event or, just as possible, although more difficult for students to see without access to other accounts, they may simply miss out negative aspects.

Asking questions

Devise an interesting and important question for pupils to investigate. For example:

■ As these sources are all taken from a parish magazine, produced by the church, do we have a reliable picture of leisure activities of the people of Appleton-Le Street in the nineteenth century?

Organising information

Ask your pupils to organise the sources into groups showing which are associated with leisure and non-leisure, with justifications for their decisions. The groups might be:

Leisure activity
The Club Feast
The Parish Tea
The Cricket Club
Prize Competition

Non-leisure activity
Organ Fund
Record of marriages/births/deaths
Magic lantern views of Calcutta

Other evidence of reliability

Ask your pupils what else they would need to know to develop a proper answer to the question of reliability. At least some of the following are significant:

■ size of the population of Appleton-le-Street

■ number and proportion of people involved in leisure activities mentioned in the parish magazine

■ account of other leisure activities in Appleton-le-Street and elsewhere in England

■ the types of people who engaged in these and other leisure activities (ie men, women, rich, poor etc)

■ an understanding of the nineteenth-century concept of leisure.

Interpreting the evidence

Was the parish tea and entertainment a success? Encourage pupils to develop two different interpretations of this event. This will help them to see that:

■ it was a poorly attended event which was dominated by performances by members of the vicar's family, and which lost money

but that

■ it did gather valuable funds which enabled children of the parish to be helped, and which was seen, at least by some, as being 'happy'.

NOTICE.—ORGAN FUND.

The Sale of Work, as before announced, will take place on July 17th, in the old Vicarage Grounds at Appleton. The gates will be opened at 2 o'clock; admission 6d. Tea will be provided in the large tent at 6d. each. It is hoped there will be as large an attendance as last year, and that the bazaar goods may prove so attractive that a sufficient sum of money may be raised and the Organ placed in Church before Christmas. The Cricket Match against Settrington will begin at 12 on the ground behind the church. The Tennis Match on the vicarage lawn will begin about 6, the winner to choose any article in the bazaar. There will be a Dance in the evening in the large tent. Messrs. H. Bradford, F. Shepherd, and T. Avison have consented to act as Stewards. Admission 6d.

THE CLUB FEAST.

After their morning meeting the members marched in procession to Church, led by the Kirbymoorside Band. After the service, which was heartily joined in, they marched back to dinner. After the very bountiful and excellent provision had been done justice to, there followed a Cricket Match—the Bradshaw Family versus the World. The Band—which deserves a special word of commendation—played under the tent during the afternoon. And at the end the World was found to have come off second best. The weather was all that could be desired.

THE PARISH TEA AND ENTERTAINMENT.

Although this was not crowded—owing partly, perhaps, to the weather, and partly to the novelty of the thing—yet it was a very happy affair. The provision was so ample that which was left sufficed to give a penny tea on the following day to over ninety children. The Entertainment was most enjoyable and much appreciated. Our best thanks are due to the performers, Miss Peach, Miss E. Peach, Miss R. Peach, Mr. E. Strickland, Mr H. Marriott, Mr. C. Channon, Mr. H. Bradford, and Mr. F. Shepherd. After the children's tea a fire balloon was sent up which travelled about two miles before falling. Total cost, £2 10s.; taken at the door, £1 19s. 7d.; deficit, 10s. 5d.

NOTICE.—ORGAN FUND.

There will be a Sale of Work at the Vicarage in July. Miss Peach hopes every one will help to make it as great a success as it was last year.

CRICKET CLUB.

The Vicar has been elected President for this year, and the Opening Match will be on Easter Monday.

GOOD FRIDAY.

Remember to keep this as a Holy Day, not a Holiday.

PRIZE COMPETITION.

i. For what several purposes was the Holy Ghost given to the Apostles? Give instances.
ii. What is the office and work of
    1. A Bishop
    2. A Priest
    3. A Deacon } in the Church of Christ.
    4. A Layman
N.B.—Not more than one prize for every two competitors will be given.

BAPTISMS.

November 10th.—Tom Prest.
   ,,   10th.—Gerty Baron.
   ,,   10th.—Violet Anne Coates.

BURIAL.

November 17th.—William Brown, of Newsham, aged 66.

MAGIC LANTERN VIEWS OF CALCUTTA.

On Saturday, November 30th, the evening of St. Andrew's Day, there will be shown, in the Upper School, at 7-30 p.m., some views of Calcutta, of the Oxford Mission House, and of the Mission School, of which the Rev. J. L. Peach is, at present, the headmaster. We shall be glad to see a large number present, and hope that after seeing those places on the "sheet" we may keep them in our minds' eye, and take still greater interest in the work done for CHRIST in that far off land.

The Borthwick Institute of Historical Research

LEFT: Extracts from the parish magazine of Appleton-le-Street in the North Riding of Yorkshire showing some of the opportunities for organised leisure in a rural village, April 1889.

RELIGION

THE BACKGROUND

Religion means different things to different people, but as far as historical research goes it means, for the most part, organised religion. It is possible to investigate the religious opinions and beliefs of some individuals, but this is not an easy task. Religious preambles to post-Reformation wills have been used extensively for this purpose. The first clause of a will usually commends the testator's soul to God and some historians have felt able to identify typically Roman Catholic and Protestant preambles.

The general availability of wills, both geographically and socially, has held out the possibility of comparative statistical work and generalisation on the basis of these typical preambles. There are, however, many problems associated with this work, including (among others) the difficulty of determining whether the preamble represents the opinions of the testator or the writer of the will, and the fact that manuals existed suggesting appropriate preambles for different levels of the social scale. As a result of these difficulties, some recent writers on the period have been sceptical about the value of this sort of work.

Diaries have also been used to investigate religious beliefs, but these are by their nature uncommon and individual sources from which it is unwise to draw general conclusions.

Up until the Reformation in the 1530s there was one organised church to which all people belonged. From the Reformation onwards the nature and basis of organised religion changed and became more diverse. At first there was a single national church of England, and efforts were made to make its membership comprehensive. Bishops of the Church of England used their old pre-Reformation powers of visitation to inspect their flocks and to prosecute offenders against the established church in their own church courts. However, these attempts failed in the face of the emergence of various strands of Protestant Nonconformity alongside the old Roman Catholic religion. The attitude of the Church of England to

Hutton Deutsch

Scripture reader in a night refuge, 1872.

Nonconformity changed, and after the Toleration Act of 1688 visitations began to be used to collect information about the strength of Recusancy and Nonconformity in each diocese rather than to prosecute offenders.

THE CONSEQUENCES

Bishops and archbishops were supposed to visit their dioceses in the first year after their enthronement (the primary visitation) and intervals every three years after that. The main records of visitations until the early eighteenth century are:

■ court books (records of prosecutions for such offences as non-attendance at divine service, non-payment of church rates and sexual offences)

■ exhibit books (which record the licences of clergymen and others to officiate in the diocese).

From the beginning of the eighteenth century, these records are supplemented by visitation returns. These are questionnaires, sent to each incumbent and returned to the bishop, asking questions about such things as the provision of education and Sunday Schools, the average numbers who attend divine service, if there are any obstacles to people attending, or whether there are any nonconformist or other places of worship within the parish. Using these records it is therefore possible to build up a picture of the state of the Church of England within a parish and in wider areas, compiled from sources devised at the time to do exactly this job.

These same sources can be used to examine the strengths or weaknesses of other churches in the same areas at the same times, from the point of view of what can be seen as their main rival.

LOCATING THE RECORDS

Visitation returns are kept with the records of the diocese that produced them. For the eighteenth and nineteenth centuries these records are now most often to be found in the relevant diocesan record office. But in the nineteenth century new dioceses were founded at an increasing rate after the foundation of the see of Ripon in 1836 (the first new see since the Reformation) to cope with the rapidly growing population and the growing threat of nonconformity and apathy. Some of these new dioceses have yet to deposit large quantities of records in their appropriate repository, so some visitation records might still be in the diocesan registry. If in doubt, the county record office is the first place to begin enquiries.

Visitation returns survive sporadically. Some can be found from the early eighteenth century, and they become fairly common in the nineteenth. Even so, it is by no means uncommon to find that a diocese well covered at the latter end of the nineteenth century has very poor coverage for the earlier period.

OTHER RECORDS

■ preambles to wills after the Reformation

■ the records of the various organised churches

■ records of the Church of England courts

■ diaries

■ newspapers

■ Quarter Sessions and diocesan records of the licensing of dissenters' meeting houses.

ACTIVITY: UNDERSTANDING EXPLANATIONS IN HISTORY

Sources are the raw material of history. When they are used they become evidence. This fine dividing line between sources and evidence becomes even harder to distinguish when one wishes to use a document to probe why a particular explanation has been given. In the extracts from the visitation return for 1865 by the vicar of Featherstone that follow it is clear that he is describing the condition of his church and parish but that he is also explaining why certain circumstances have arisen. Pupils need to be encouraged to read between the lines of such sources to understand why and how an explanation or interpretation has been reached. The factors to consider are:

■ To what extent is the explanation related to the nature of the individual who has written the report. In this particular case the vicar is 79 years old and he has 'performed the whole duty' for 'nearly 40 years'. Is this the sign of great experience, knowledge and understanding or has this been mentioned in such a way to make us believe that he is embittered and the views that follow will be rather jaundiced?

■ Is the format of the report likely to influence the development of the explanation that is given? The visitation return was an official instrument which allowed the church to be prepared for the inspection that would take place. If the person completing the form was concerned to make a good impression the comments in the report are likely to be stated in a very positive light. Or the writer might wish to lower the expectations of the person who would eventually visit the parish and so encourage sympathy for the difficulties faced by the vicar.

■ What factors does the writer draw attention to in the report? Attention to this matter will give the pupils the opportunity to consider the broader context in which the report has been constructed. Is the area inhabited by particular types of people? Has the area seen

any recent changes, and if so what has caused those changes? Is it reasonable for the writer to present these external factors in this way? Is it really true for example that the establishment of an evening school would mean only that it was 'a pearl before....' (swine)?

Other records would need to be consulted to be able to reach a proper understanding of many of these issues. What are reports like from similar (perhaps neighbouring) parishes?

■ Does the report have internal

consistency? In other words, does the vicar seem to express the same sort of views about similar issues, or does he contradict himself, or at least have a range of views?

■ Are the issues that are raised in the report all of equal significance in relation to the historical question that is under consideration? For example, if a question was being asked about the condition of the parish, would it be possible to establish a hierarchy of factors which would help develop an explanation?

The Borthwick Institute of Historical Research

EDUCATION

Until the reforms of the 1870s (especially the Acts of 1870, 1876 and 1880), the provision of education at all levels was patchy and attendance was not compulsory even at elementary (primary) school. As a result, only a minority of schools at elementary level, and even fewer at secondary level, can boast histories earlier than the second half of the nineteenth century. This does not mean, however, that there is nothing to discover before then. Private schools might be noted in trades directories and newspapers, (grammar) schoolmasters' nominations can be found amongst diocesan records back to the seventeenth century.

Some work on literacy levels can be done by using, for example, the signatures and marks on wills and probate bonds (using bonds gets round the obvious problem of a literate person on his or her death bed not being able to hold a pen properly) and from 1754 in marriage registers. Of course, an inability to write a name does not equal illiteracy - reading is a different skill that cannot be measured by writing. For a large number (though still a minority) of elementary schools, the archives of the National Society hold information from the early nineteenth century.

THE CONSEQUENCES
The reforms of the 1870s mark the beginning of the provision of education at elementary level on a national basis. As a result, documentation is much more common and might still be available in school. The archivist in your local record office will be able to advise on depositing archives in the appropriate repository and making selected copies for use in school.

There is a wide variety of documents about school buildings, school administration, pupils and teaching methods which are easily available.

SCHOOL BUILDINGS
You may come across the following types of document which can help trace the history of a school building:

Mike Corbishley

Faunce Street School, Kennington around 1910.

■ Architects' plans

■ Inventories of school equipment. In 1903 responsibility for schools passed from School Boards to the County Council. Most councils listed exactly what they now owned.

■ Surveyors' reports

■ Photographs.

Information about the building, its fixtures and its equipment will be particularly useful if you want to carry out any costumed drama and role play.

SCHOOL ADMINISTRATION
Documents to investigate to show the administration of the school are:

■ Log books

■ Minute books

■ School accounts

■ School rule books

■ School magazines

■ Newspaper cuttings.

Log books
Of these documents listed above the school log book will probably yield the most interesting informa-

tion. The principal teacher was required to make an entry at least once a week, specifying ordinary progress and other facts concerning the school or its teachers - such as the dates of withdrawal, commencements of duty, cautions or illnesses. Examples of the sort of information recorded in log books are:

■ Names of staff and managers Salaries paid to staff / Inspectors' reports

■ Names of individual pupils Late arrival, truancy, misdemeanours and punishments

■ Details of equipment and textbooks / Lesson outlines

■ Programmes of school concerts and other entertainment

■ Medical information about epidemics / Comments on the weather

■ Information about holidays for harvests, fairs and national events / National and international events which affected the routines of school life

■ Records of pupils who passed examinations or who won prizes

■ Significant events in the life of the school.

ACTIVITY: LOG BOOKS

Yearly survey
Choose a particular week. Collect together significant items from the log book in that week over a period of time. Make an analysis of change and continuity over the period. Are there any connections between the activities of children in the past and those at school today?

Epidemic
Find an account of an epidemic in the school. Take on the role of the medical officer of health. What makes you decide to close the school or to leave it open?

Lifelines
Draw a chronology of the events in the life of one of the head teachers who stayed at the school for some time. Beside it, record some of the major events which were happening elsewhere in the world at the same time.

Boys and girls
Compare entries which feature boys and male teachers and entries which feature females. Are there any differences?

PUPILS
A great deal of information about pupils can be gleaned from log books but you may also investigate:

■ Admissions registers

■ Class and pupil photographs

■ Certificates of attendance, sports and merit

■ School reports.

ACTIVITY: ADMISSIONS REGISTERS
Data about pupils listed in admission registers can be analysed in various ways:

First names - comparing them with the most popular names today.

Surnames - linking members of a family through the register and reaching conclusions about family size in the past.

Log book entries from the records of a primary school

School closes this afternoon, for organised picking of Blackberries, in accordance with Board of Education Circular 1056. — 1918

Av. att. Mixed = 79.4   Infants = 30.1
Gerald & Joyce Gladwell, are excluded owing to Ringworm. — 1919

Owing to parts of ceiling having given way, with consequent danger to children, School closes this afternoon, for repairs. — 1921

Nurse Wallace called with reference to Dorothy Drycraft, excluded on 3 March, verminous — still in the same state this morning — sent home by School Nurse, again. — 1922

For dinner today only boiled potatoes & rice arrived. — 1944

School did not meet today — being the occasion of the cessation of hostilities in Europe. — 1945

Great Oakley Primary School

List of Object lessons for Infants & Stan: I
1. A Brick.
2. A Book.
3. India-rubber ball.
4. A School slate.
5. A knife & fork.
16. Coal.
17. A barrel and a bucket.
18. A table.
19. A tallow-candle.
20. Leather.

St. Mary's Church School, Huntingfield, Suffolk

ABOVE: Object lesson text from a school log book, 1898.

Age of pupils admitted - what changes have taken place since then?

Catchment area - carrying out a mapping exercise to compare catchment areas, then and now. Finding out how pupils did or might have got to school.

TEACHING METHODS
Teaching methods may be examined through various documents, including some already mentioned. For example, pupils sitting neatly at their desks for the class photograph and the ratio of pupils to teachers gives some indication of teaching methods and styles. Other, more specific, documents which can be consulted are:

■ Object lessons (either printed or included in the school log book)

■ School inspectors' reports

■ Punishment books

■ Exercise and text books

■ Teaching and learning aids, such as maps and charts.

THEMES IN CONTEXT

The other sections in this book adopt a themed approach, with an underlying assumption that most teachers will study these themes in the context of particular places. Each of the themes constitutes a satisfying study in its own right, but they can also be put together to create a more rounded history of an individual area. Any 'localised history' needs to be as rooted in the locality itself as it is in documents and secondary works. The physical evidence of the locality should be used in conjunction with the documentary evidence. Buildings - their age, style, size and location - are telling pointers to the development of places and to the changes they undergo. The alignment of roads, the size and shape of fields and other features can all yield important and interesting evidence.

MAPS

Where recent development overlies older features, it is nearly always possible to discover something of the earlier landscape, whether urban or rural, through maps. The Ordnance Survey began to map the whole country on the scale of 1 inch to 1 mile at the very beginning of the nineteenth century. In the 1850s much more detailed maps, at 6 inches to the mile, were produced in Lancashire and Yorkshire, with the rest of the country following later. Some lucky towns were mapped at the enormously detailed scale of 5 feet to the mile in the middle of the century. In the 1890s the Ordnance Survey mapped the whole country at 25 inches to the mile, so that every place should have a detailed map which is at least 100 years old.

Tithe maps

As well as general coverage provided by the Ordnance Survey, most (though not all) places have a large scale manuscript tithe map dated between 1836 and 1850. These maps were drawn up as a result of the Tithe Commutation Act of 1836. Tithe awards were drawn up at the same time as the maps. These awards give the names of landowners and occupiers/tenants, field/property names, the state of cultivation and area of each field or property, together with a note of how much tithe was payable and to whom.

Enclosure and estate maps

In many places there are similar maps from an earlier date, drawn up under the Enclosure Acts of the eighteenth and nineteenth centuries. These maps vary greatly in standard and detail, but are always informative and were also accompanied by awards.

Estate maps can be dated even earlier. There are very few of these for the medieval period - around 100 nationally. However, from the end of the sixteenth century they become more common. Their existence depends on whether a particular area was part of a landed estate. The maps themselves were drawn for a variety of purposes. A new or improving landlord might require one, as might the sale of an estate. Estate maps vary in quality, some being detailed and all inclusive, others being little more than amateur sketches.

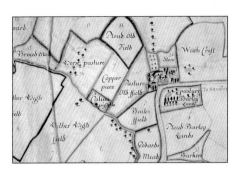

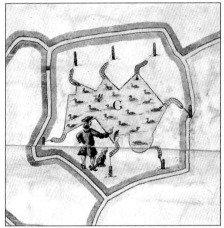

TOP: Estate map of Goddard's Farm, Thaxted, Essex 1706.

ABOVE RIGHT: Decorative interpretation of a duck-decoy from an estate map of Tillingham, Essex 1739.

RIGHT: Two surveyors with theodolite and measuring rod: decorative detail from an estate map of Pebmarsh, Essex 1807.

BELOW: Detail from a tithe map of 1839 for Great Oakley, Essex.

Essex Record Office

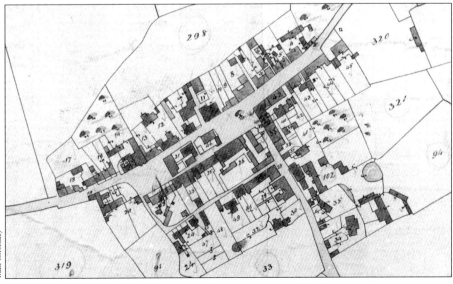

Mike Corbishley

CASE STUDY: BUCKMINSTER

This case study looks at the buildings, maps and other sources for Buckminster in Leicestershire. It is taken from a survey of three Leicestershire villages carried out by the Buckminster and District Local History Research Group. Their work (see Bibliography) was a result of local history classes organised by the Workers' Educational Association. You may find similar research work in your area.

Accessible documents

Many of the documents which you will want to use for the study of a locality will be accessible, easily, in libraries and local history centres or in district or county record offices. Apart from maps the most important documents referred to were:

- Trades directories
- Census Returns
- Auction notices with inventories
- Photographs (especially those made into postcards in the late nineteenth and early twentieth centuries)
- School log books
- Newspaper accounts.

Brickyard Close (ABOVE): The tithe award map of 1841 shows this area pockmarked with ponds created by the digging of clay. The census return of 1841 lists Charles Hopkins and Thomas Parkinson as brickmakers. The sale notice for 11 June 1873 says,

"At the Buckminster Brick Yard the property of Mr Henson, Hovel boards, Planks, Brick Press, Well Sinking Frame, eight centres nine feet long, three Morticed Posts and Rails, 1000 Bundles of Reeds, Pantiles, Ridge Tiles and Bricks, quantity of Firewood and numerous effects."

Buckminster Institute (ABOVE): The Institute "for the benefit of the working men of Buckminster and the surrounding villages" was founded in 1886 and paid for by the Earl of Dysart. The Institute had a large playroom with billiards, bagatelle, draughts and dominoes; a reading room with London and provincial newspapers, a library of 250 books and a table and writing materials; a committee room and caretaker's quarters. The annual subscription was 5s "but the committee have the power to admit lads and labourers at 1d per week".

The Crescent: Houses built in 1892 replaced Bull Row which was built in the early 1830s. The census return for 1851 lists 166 people living here.

RIGHT: It is possible to make connections between documentary evidence and the evidence of buildings and landscapes. The Workers' Educational Association group was able to put together a map of Buckminster village for 1885 based on documentary evidence and observation on the ground.

Buckminster.

GENTRY.

Dysart Right Hon. Earl, Buckminster Hall
Lawson Rev. James, M.A. [vicar]

TRADERS.

Adcock John, 'Blue Cow,' baker & farmer
Ash George, butcher & shopkeeper
Bartram Richard, chairmaker
Bartram William, chairmaker
Beardsell Edward, grocer, seedsman, & agent to the East of England life assurance
Benson William, brick & tile maker
Brown John, tailor, & linen & woollen draper
Brown Richard, tailor
Burton John, bailiff to Earl Dysart
Coulson Thomas, cabinet maker
Exton John, farmer & grazier
Glassup Joseph, farmer & grazier
Hack William & Robert, farmers
Hand Thomas, farmer
Hill John, bricklayer

Hill Joseph, bricklayer
Manners Alfd. agent to Earl Dysart
Marshall Arthur, farmer & grazier
Marshall John, grazier
North Henry, 'Blue Bull,' & veterinary surgeon
Sharpe Southern, butcher
Spencer John, farmer & grazier
Stevens Thomas, boot & shoe maker, & shopkeeper
Watchorn Timothy, blacksmith
Weston Thos. saddler & harness maker
Woollerton William, boot & shoe maker

Sewstern.

Atter William, esq
Holmes Rev. Henry Courtley, M.A

TRADERS.

Almond John, cattle dealer
Bartram John, chairmaker
Bartram Joseph, carrier
Bowder William, farmer & grazier
Bright Benjamin Priestman, grocer
Burrows Wm.' Waggon & Horses,' & frmr
Challand John, 'Red Lion'
Christain Esther (Mrs.), grazier

Christain Robert, farmer & grazier
Cramp William, carpenter
Doubleday Henry, farmer
Doubleday John, farmer
Dunmore William, carrier
Exton Thomas, farmer & grazier
Grice John, cattle dealer
Grice Mary (Mrs.), farmer
Grice Richard, 'Blue Dog'
Hardy John, grocer
Harvey Thomas, tailor & draper
Harvey William, shoemaker
Herring Thomas, farmer & grazier
North Joseph, blacksmith
Parker Mary (Mrs.), shopkeeper
Remington John, farmer
Robinson Samuel, boot & shoe maker
Royce Joseph, farmer & grazier
Royce Mark, horse dealer & farmer
Smith Thorpe, miller & baker
Thraves Samuel, tailor
Tinkler William, grazier
Townsend George, carpenter
Ward John, farmer
Wormell Mary (Mrs.), shopkeeper

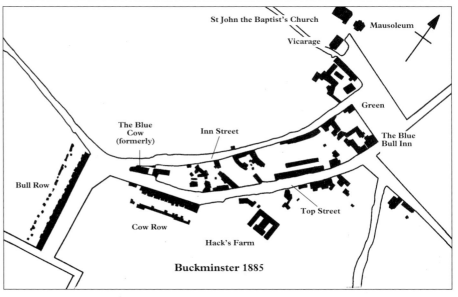

St John the Baptist's Church
Mausoleum
Vicarage
Green
The Blue Cow (formerly)
Inn Street
The Blue Bull Inn
Bull Row
Top Street
Cow Row
Hack's Farm

Buckminster 1885

English Heritage Education Service

Ivy House (LEFT): Now a private house, this was once a public house called The Blue Bull. Kelly's Post Office Directory of 1855 lists the landlord as Henry North and records that he was also a veterinary surgeon. The Blue Bull's licence was allowed to lapse at the wish of the Earl of Dysart, the local squire who owned the entire village. Its auction catalogue contains a detailed inventory of each room and store.

Buckminster School (ABOVE): This school building was completed in 1899 on a new site opposite the former school. The Earl of Dysart paid for its construction and it was named 'The Buckminster Unsectarian School'.

Analysing the documents

An analysis of the trades directories can give a useful insight into the trades and professions in one locality. In census returns years the two documents may be compared. The Workers' Educational Association group analysed the census return for 1851, see below.

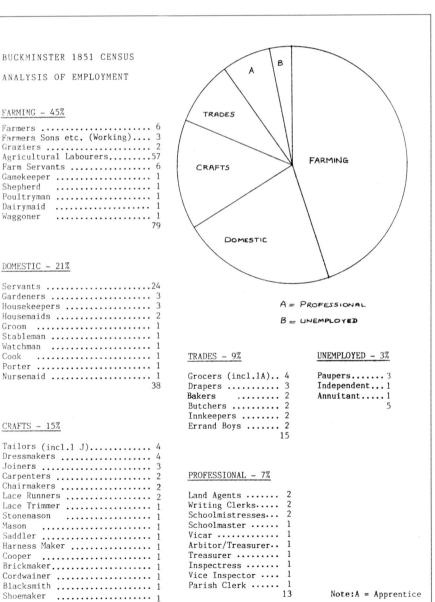

```
BUCKMINSTER 1851 CENSUS

ANALYSIS OF EMPLOYMENT


FARMING - 45%

Farmers ...................... 6
Farmers Sons etc. (Working).... 3
Graziers ..................... 2
Agricultural Labourers........57
Farm Servants ................ 6
Gamekeeper ................... 1
Shepherd   ................... 1
Poultryman ................... 1
Dairymaid .................... 1
Waggoner   ................... 1
                            79


DOMESTIC - 21%

Servants .....................24
Gardeners .................... 3
Housekeepers ................. 3
Housemaids ................... 2
Groom  ....................... 1
Stableman .................... 1
Watchman ..................... 1
Cook   ....................... 1
Porter ....................... 1
Nursemaid .................... 1
                            38


CRAFTS - 15%

Tailors (incl.1 J)............ 4
Dressmakers .................. 4
Joiners ...................... 3
Carpenters ................... 2
Chairmakers .................. 2
Lace Runners ................. 2
Lace Trimmer ................. 1
Stonemason ................... 1
Mason  ....................... 1
Saddler ...................... 1
Harness Maker ................ 1
Cooper ....................... 1
Brickmaker.................... 1
Cordwainer ................... 1
Blacksmith ................... 1
Shoemaker  ................... 1
                            27
```

Pie chart labels: A, B, TRADES, CRAFTS, FARMING, DOMESTIC

A = PROFESSIONAL
B = UNEMPLOYED

```
TRADES - 9%

Grocers (incl.1A).. 4
Drapers .......... 3
Bakers   ......... 2
Butchers ......... 2
Innkeepers ....... 2
Errand Boys ...... 2
                15


PROFESSIONAL - 7%

Land Agents ....... 2
Writing Clerks..... 2
Schoolmistresses... 2
Schoolmaster ...... 1
Vicar ............. 1
Arbitor/Treasurer.. 1
Treasurer ........ 1
Inspectress ...... 1
Vice Inspector .... 1
Parish Clerk ..... 1
                13
```

```
UNEMPLOYED - 3%

Paupers........ 3
Independent...1
Annuitant.....1
             5
```

Note:A = Apprentice

J = Journeyman

The Green (ABOVE): This is still the place for the annual Buckminster Festival. An annual village feast was held on the Sunday after 6 July. The annual 'club day' of the local Buckminster Friendly Society turned into another feast day for the whole village from the 1850s. There was a church service and processions led by village bands from the area around. In 1859 the local Grantham Journal reported:

"In the evening the members paraded the village, the Band playing at most of the principal houses where they were regaled with plenty of 'Sir John Barleycorn'. All passed off quietly excepting one instance. A poor imbecile musician of the violin tribe who annoyed the people by performing the part of 'Punch and Judy' got so drunk and abusive that he was obliged to be waited on by a gentleman in blue."

Levi Briggs from the village of Skillington was charged with drunkenness and fined 5s.

DOCUMENTS ACROSS THE CURRICULUM

Using documents can bring together different curriculum areas. You should choose appropriate and manageable links between subjects.

ENGLISH

Through documents it is possible to develop the skills of speaking and listening, and reading and writing. In their responses to documents pupils can be encouraged to understand how the vocabulary and grammar of standard English has developed. They will listen and respond to others' interpretations of documents, and formulate their own ideas. They must be able to read fluently and intelligently, employing the skills, for example, of synthesis and evaluation. An understanding of the phrasing of documents for particular audiences will be developed.

MATHEMATICS

Data handling can be used extensively with pupils collecting, representing and analysing, and interpreting. It would be valuable for pupils to estimate and calculate the probabilities of events on the basis of numerical data shown in documents with the 'answer' being supplied later by the teacher who could show the next table of information.

SCIENCE

This subject allows pupils to establish systematic enquiries which explain the nature of scientific ideas and how they may be applied. Good communication skills should be developed and ideas and practices related to health and safety should be promoted. Many of the documents used here cater for this sort of work.

DESIGN AND TECHNOLOGY

Certain practical skills associated with Design and Technology may be developed through a study of documents. Pupils are often instructed to use documents as a guide to the creation of a particular

THE CROQUET LAWN, BEAUMONT HALL, CLACTON-ON-SEA.

Norman Jacobs

A game of croquet in about 1903. Old postcard pictures are a readily accessible source of evidence, which may be collected from pupils' families or be found in published sources.

object. Before, during and after construction pupils could comment on the usefulness of the way in which those written and diagrammatic instructions have been framed.

INFORMATION TECHNOLOGY

Pupils should use IT to organise, reorganise and analyse ideas and information gained from documents (for example, census returns). They should check the plausibility of the information provided by documents. It will be possible for them to undertake exercises involving controlling, monitoring and modelling data.

HISTORY

As all the documents used in this book are from the past it is immediately obvious that pupils will be able to develop understanding in all the key areas of the National Curriculum and other frameworks. A sense of chronology, a range and depth of historical knowledge and understanding, interpretations of history, enquiry skills and the ability to organise and communicate information appropriately are all potentially fruitful areas.

GEOGRAPHY

The understanding of place in both its physical and human dimensions is dependent upon documents. Documents other than maps (for example, census returns and parish registers) allow pupils to ask centrally important geographical questions such as What/where is it? What is it like? How did it get like this? Thematic studies which look, for example, at the quality of the environment, demand an appreciation of the knowledge made available largely through documents.

ART

Pictorial work is not usually thought of as coming within the definition of a document, although there is no reason why a study of, for example, nineteenth-century Punch cartoons as compared with modern illustrative work could not be undertaken. The different ways that artists have worked over time and the ways that they have chosen to communicate their ideas is something which can be taught through documents.

BIBLIOGRAPHY AND RESOURCES

TEACHING AND LEARNING HISTORY

Andreeti, K, **Teaching History from Primary Evidence**, David Fulton, 1993.
ISBN 1-85346-183-0.

Bourdillon, H, (ed), **Teaching History**, Routledge in association with the Open University, 1994.
ISBN 0-415-10256-1. See in particular part 3 and John Fines' chapter 'Evidence: the basis of the discipline'.

Brown, R, **Managing the Learning of History**, David Fulton, 1995.
ISBN 1-85346-345-0.

Cooper, H, **The Teaching of History**, David Fulton, 1992.
ISBN 1-85346-186-5. Concentrates on the way in which primary school pupils think when studying history.

Dickinson, A K and Lee, P J (eds) **History Teaching and Historical Understanding**, Heinemann, 1978.
ISBN 0-435-80291-7.

Dickinson, A K, Lee, P J and Rogers P J, (eds), **Learning History**, Heinemann, 1984. ISBN 0-435-80289-5.

Dickinson, A K and Lee, P J, **Investigating Progression in Children's Ideas about History: the CHATA project**, 1994 in John, P and Lucas, P (eds), **Partnership and Progress: new developments in History teacher education and History teaching**, University of Sheffield, USDE Papers in Education 17.
ISBN 0-902831-29-1.

Farmer, A and Knight, P, **Active History in Key Stages 3 and 4**, David Fulton, 1995.
ISBN 1-85346-305-1.

Hake, C and Hadyn, T, **Stories or Sources**, 1995 in Teaching History, Historical Association No 78 January 1995, pp 20-22.

Knight, P, **Primary Geography, Primary History**, David Fulton, 1995. ISBN 1-85346-207-1.

Lomas, T, **Teaching and Assessing Historical Understanding**, 1990, Teaching of History series No 63. The Historical Association.
ISBN 0-85278-317-5.

Palmer, M and Batho, G, **The Source Method in History Teaching**, 1983, Teaching of History series No 48, The Historical Association.
ISBN 0-85278-237-3.

Portal, C, (ed), **The History Curriculum for Teachers**, The Falmer Press, 1987.
ISBN 1-85000-166-9.

Sebba, J, **History for All**, David Fulton, 1995.
ISBN 1-85346-306-X.

Shemilt, D, **History 13-16 Evaluation Study**, Holmes McDougall, 1980.
ISBN 0-7157-2017-1.

Southern Regional Examinations Board, Sources in history: from definition to assessment, 1987.

Teaching History Research Group, **How to plan teaching and assessment of history in the National Curriculum**, Heinemann, 1991, pp 80-85. ISBN 0-435-31072-0.

Watts, R and Grosvenor, I, (eds), **Crossing the Key Stages of History: effective teaching 5-16 and beyond**, David Fulton, 1995.
ISBN 1-85346-324-8.

DOCUMENTS AND RECORDS

Braithwaite, L, **Exploring British Cities**, A & C Black, 1986. ISBN 0-7136-2748-4. A guide to the historic buildings in twenty-nine British cities using nineteenth-century Ordnance Survey maps as a base.

Clinton, D, **When Bacon was Sixpence a Pound: Victorian Life in Buckminster, Sewstern and Sproxton**, Workers Educational Association, 1989.

Dymond, D, **Writing Local History: A Practical Guide**, British Association for Local History* (BALH), 1988. ISBN

Evans, E, **Tithes, Maps, Apportionments and the 1836 Act**, BALH, 1993.
ISBN 0-85033-857-3.

Grace, F, **The Late Victorian Town**, BALH, 1991.
ISBN 0-85033-712-7.

Munby, L, **Reading Tudor and Stuart Handwriting**, BALH, 1988. ISBN 0-85033-638-4.

Munby, L, **How much is that worth?**, BALH, 1989.
ISBN 0-85033-741-0.

Murphy, M, **Newspapers and Local History**, BALH, 1991.
ISBN 0-85033-782-8.

Norrington, V, **Recording the Present**, BALH, 1989. ISBN 0-85033-709-7.

Reid, A, **The Union Workhouse**, BALH, 1994. ISBN 0-85033-914-6.

Stephens, W B, **Sources for English Local History**, Cambridge University Press, 1981 (2nd edition). ISBN 0-521-28213-6. The most useful guide to records.

Gibson's Guides for Genealogists are as useful to local historians as they are to genealogists. Each book covers a particular source, with a short introduction to the nature of the records followed by a much longer gazetteer of the availability of holdings throughout the country, for example: Census Returns 1841-1891 in microform, a directory to local holdings in Great Britain; Local Census Listings 1522-1930, holdings in the British Isles; Marriage, Census and other indexes for family historians. All titles are cheaply-priced and available by post from The Federation of Family History Societies, c/o Benson Room, Birmingham and Midland Institute, Margaret Street, Birmingham BS3 3BS.

* The British Association for Local History promotes local history by giving support to those interested. There is an annual conference and publications which are helpful to teachers. For more information contact: Ashwell Education Services, Merchant Taylor's House, Ashwell, Baldock, Hertfordshire SG7 5LY. Ashwell Education

Services publish a *Teaching Local History* series and two titles are currently available: Medieval Life, The Victorians. Roman Life, The Tudors, The Second World War and The New Poor Law are in preparation.

Record offices
For addresses of record offices and brief summaries of their holdings the standard work is:
Foster, J and Sheppard, J, **British Archives: a guide to archive resources in the United Kingdom,** Macmillan, 1995. ISBN 0-333-532-534. You will find copies of this reference book in most record offices and many local history libraries.

Archive packs
Many record offices have published archive packs about topics and themes in their own area. They are always good value for schools with both large size copies of records, maps and photographs and detailed background information. Some record offices have produced supplementary material written especially for teachers and pupils. See also:
Cross, T and Gosling, N, **The Great War 1914-18: a practical workshop for 7-11 year olds in Teaching History**, The Historical Association, No 46 October 1986, pp 28-33. A report of work undertaken using a document pack.
Overy, C, **The Peabody Trust Document Pack**, English Heritage, 1995.
Palmer, M, **Archive Packs for Schools: some practical suggestions** in **Journal of the Society of Archivists** Vol 6 No 3, pp 145-153.

BOOKS FOR PUPILS
Calwell, I, Culpin, C, Shephard, C and Shuter, P, **Using Historical Sources**, Heinemann, 1990. ISBN 0-435-31045-3.
Hinton, C, **What is Evidence?**, John Murray, 1990. ISBN 0-7195-4733-4.
Macdonald, C K, **Using Evidence**, Basil Blackwell, 1986. ISBN 0-631-900217.
May, C, **Evidence and Investigations**, Hodder and Stoughton, 1990. ISBN 0-340-519315.
Pearce, M L, **Sources in History: 20th Century**, Bell and Hyman, 1986.

ISBN 0-7135-2625-4.
Richardson, J, **Looking at Local Records**, Batsford, 1983. ISBN 0-7134-3664-6.

EDUCATIONAL APPROACHES
English Heritage has about 40 handbooks for teachers to encourage the curriculum use of individual sites and monuments. Each handbook contains a section on documents which relate to the site. The series *Education on Site* suggests educational strategies for using the historic environment. The titles listed below all include a number of documentary sources and how to use them in curriculum work.
Alderton, D, **Using industrial sites**, 1995. ISBN 1-85074-445-9.
Barnicoat, J, **Newspapers and conservation**, 1994. ISBN 1-85074-511-0.
Cooksey, C, **Using abbeys**, 1992. ISBN 1-85074-328-2.
Copeland, T, **Using castles**, 1993. ISBN 1-85074-327-4.
Durbin, G, **Using historic houses**, 1993. ISBN 1-85074-390-8.
Fairclough, J, **History through role play**, 1994. ISBN 1-85074-478-5.
Keith, C, **Using listed buildings**, 1991. ISBN 1-85074-297-9.
Marcus, S and Barker, R, **Using historic parks and gardens**, forthcoming 1996. ISBN 1-85074-510-2.
Planel, P, **Battlefields, defence, conflict and warfare**, 1995. ISBN 1-85074-590-0.
Purkis, S, **Using school buildings**, 1993. ISBN 1-85074-379-7.
Purkis, S, **Using memorials**, 1995. ISBN 1-85074-493-9.

VIDEOS
English Heritage have produced a number of videos for curriculum use, both by pupils and teachers. The following videos contain sections about the use of documents in historical and archaeological research:
Archaeology at work. This series introduces to Key Stage 2 & 3 pupils the methods and the equipment used by archaeologists today, from fieldwork to documentary research to scientific techniques. **Investigating towns**, 30 minutes, 1994.

Looking for the past/Uncovering the past, 58 minutes, 1994.

Doorstep discovery - working on a local history study, 30 minutes, 1993. This video, for initial teacher training and in-service training, follows a group of teacher training students as they carry out a local history study of their own college and its immediate area. They research the buildings, documents and oral history. It then follows two students on teaching practice as they put theory into practice at a primary school.

Acknowledgements
The authors and editor would like to thank English Martyrs' Roman Catholic Primary School and Queen Anne's School, York, the Cumbria (Kendal), and Wigan Record Offices, York Health Archives, Sallie Purkis (information on school documents), illustrated maps on p31 courtesy of The Essex Record Office and Douglas Clinton and Jill McPherson (Buckminster material). The first sections of this book draws heavily on work with teachers and thinking of Paul Shuter and Neil Thompson.

OPPOSITE: Posed studio photograph of a boy from the London slums in about 1860. (Hulton Deutsch)

Our Education Service aims to help teachers at all levels make better use of the resource of the historic environment. Educational groups can make free visits to over 400 historic properties cared for by English Heritage. The following booklets are free on request. **Free Educational Visits**, **Using the Historic Environment**. Our **Resources** catalogue is also available. Please contact:

English Heritage Education Service 429 Oxford Street London W1R 2HD

Tel: 0171 973 3442 Fax: 0171 973 3443